LORI PECKHAM, editor

PATHFINDER · JUNIOR
BOOK CLUB

Guide's Greatest

HOPE
STORIES

Pacific Press®
Publishing Association

Nampa, Idaho | Oshawa, Ontario, Canada
www.pacificpress.com

Library of Congress Cataloging-in-Publication Data
Names: Peckham, Lori, editor.
Title: Guide's greatest hope stories / Lori Peckham, editor.
Description: Nampa : Pacific Press Publishing Association, 2018.
Identifiers: LCCN 2017053886 | ISBN 9780816363650 (pbk. : alk. paper)
Subjects: LCSH: Christian life—Seventh-Day Adventists authors—Juvenile literature.
   | Faith—Juvenile literature. | Hope—Religious aspects—Seventh-Day Adventists—
   Juvenile literature.
Classification: LCC BX6155 .G85 2018 | DDC 242/.62—dc23 LC record available at
   https://lccn.loc.gov/2017053886

December 2017

Contents

Also edited by Lori Peckham:

A special thanks to the authors we were unable to locate. If anyone can provide knowledge of their current mailing address, please relay this information to Lori Peckham, in care of Pacific Press® Publishing Association.

Dedication

To all those who (like me) have lost loved ones and hope for the resurrection and the new earth.

Acknowledgments

Special thanks to Kathy Beagles, Laura Sámano, and Tonya Ball, the talented and hope-filled *Guide* staff who encourage and support this project, as well as produce a life-changing weekly magazine.

"You are my hope, O Lord GOD; You are my trust from my youth" (Psalm 71:5).

Camp Meeting Grasshoppers

by J. C. Michalenko

He's a crazy fool!" That's what the neighbors called my dad the year he went to camp meeting and left our farm to be eaten by grasshoppers.

But Dad just shrugged his shoulders. And when it was all over, we found that the crazy people were the ones living on the other side of the fence! But I'm getting ahead of my story.

When I was a boy our family lived on a farm. Dad raised grain. It was a good clean crop, and when things turned out well, we were fairly well fixed for cash.

The trouble was that things didn't turn out well very often. There are so many elements that can spoil a grain crop. There's wind, for instance, and rain. Too much rain at the wrong time can keep the grain from ripening properly. Not enough rain will dry it out and shrivel it up. A hailstorm can flatten a field in no time at all. And then there are snowstorms and diseases and worms—and low prices. Any time we would get a fairly good crop, the other farmers would get good crops, too, so the grain wouldn't bring much at the market.

But, perhaps worst of all, there are the grasshoppers.

I never will forget the year they invaded our fields at harvesttime. For a whole twelve months we had been working on that crop, and then, just as we were getting ready to gather it, the grasshoppers came. They swept through our fields by the millions, eating up everything we had worked so hard to grow.

Dad jumped into action fast. "Quick, boys," he ordered. "We must harvest immediately, even though it's early."

How hard we worked those next few days! But when we were all through, we had much less grain than we would have had if it had not been for the grasshoppers.

Dad was cheerful about it, though. "We ought to be contented," he said. "We got our seed back, we have plenty of hay for our horses and cattle, and there is some extra grain we can sell too. My credit is good at the bank for a loan, and next year I'm sure we will have better success."

But the next year the grasshoppers came earlier. And if there were millions of them the previous year, there were hundreds of millions this year. All the little babies that had hatched from the eggs those grasshoppers had laid had grown up, and they must have called in their friends from miles away to attend the feast.

What could we do? Some of the neighbors ran

around with rakes and shovels and hoes, trying to heap the insects up in piles. But what good was that against a hundred million grasshoppers?

Other neighbors spread poisoned bran around the edges of their fields, hoping that the insects would eat it and kill themselves off. But most of the grasshoppers just flew over the bran and went on destroying the grain as if the poison wasn't there.

My father did what he could, but he didn't have much time to attend to grasshoppers. It was camp meeting time, and Mother and Dad hadn't missed a camp meeting in years and years. They didn't intend to miss this year either, grasshoppers or no grasshoppers.

When the neighbors heard about it, they couldn't believe their ears. "Have you heard of the foolish thing Peter Michalenko's planning to do?" one would ask another. "He's going off to some religious meetings somewhere, and he's going to leave his crops for the grasshoppers to eat."

"Ha, ha, ha," the neighbors would laugh. "That's the silliest thing we've heard of yet."

One of the neighbors, however, perhaps more friendly than the rest, came to Dad to find out if it was really true.

"Peter," he said, "don't you think you're unwise to leave your fields at the mercy of the grasshoppers while you are at camp meeting more than one hundred fifty miles away?"

But my dad knew what he was doing. "Friend," he answered, "I am in partnership with God. He will take care of my crops. You see, over there in the Good Book, God says, 'I will rebuke the devourer for your sakes, and he shall not destroy the fruits of your ground' [Malachi 3:11, KJV]."

"But," the friend spluttered, "how can you believe *that* when the grasshoppers are already here, eating your grain?"

It was a tough question. I'll have to admit I was having a pretty hard time trying to believe that promise myself.

Dad only smiled, however. "Friend," he said, "you'll see someday. Perhaps the grasshoppers will eat some of our grain, but God will take care of us. We'll come out all right in the end."

The neighbor shook his head and walked off. And Dad went on with his preparations for camp meeting.

I had to stay home the first part of the meetings to take care of the necessary chores. I saw the grasshoppers everywhere. They would fly out from under my feet as I went from the house to the barn. They crawled over the screens on the windows. They bumped against my clothes when I walked through the yard.

I kept thinking of that promise Dad had quoted about God rebuking the devourer. It didn't look as though God was keeping it very well. And then I thought of some of the other promises in the Bible. Could I believe in them any better?

One day, soon after Dad had left for the camp-ground, I overheard two of the neighbors talking to each other. I wouldn't have listened to what they were saying, for that would have been rude. But when I suddenly heard one of them mention the name of Peter, I immediately was all ears. What were they saying about my father behind his back?

"That crazy fool Peter," one of them said. "He thinks that by praying at camp meeting, God will save his crops from these grasshoppers."

I didn't like that at all, I can tell you. What right did they have to call my dad a crazy fool? I felt like running up to them and asking them who they thought they were to talk about him like that. But I thought better of it and kept still. After all, I had been thinking some of the same kind of thoughts myself.

Perhaps Dad was crazy, just as those men said.

Just before it was time for me to head off to camp meeting, I thought I noticed less grasshoppers than there had been before. Eagerly I ran here and there through the fields, searching. It was true. The grasshoppers had gone—and my dad had not been there to chase them away!

Thinking some long, long thoughts, I went to the meetings. I still wasn't convinced by any means that Dad was right. There could have been any number of reasons why those grasshoppers had left, and the chief reason, no doubt, was that they had eaten all the grain we had.

Harvesttime came a few weeks later. Our neighbor harvested his fields before we did. He had a poor little pile of grain when he got through. He had fought those grasshoppers tooth and nail, but they had done tremendous damage in spite of him.

Then he came over to help Dad bring in our grain. His particular job was to haul the grain away from the threshing machine. We noticed that he kept climbing to the top of the machine to look at the indicator that told how many bushels of grain had been harvested.

After he had examined the indicator yet another time, he climbed down and walked up to my father. "I can't understand it," he said. "You are getting twice as many bushels of grain per acre as I got off my fields. What did you do to get such a good crop?"

I don't know whether Dad wanted to say "I told you so." I know what I would have said! But Dad was always tactful and polite, and he answered our neighbor as if he had never discussed the problem with him before.

"It's this way, friend," he said. "I pay tithe on all my increase, and I believed God would keep the promise He made to tithe payers, over in Malachi, chapter three. God said, 'I will rebuke the devourer for your sakes.' I guess this good crop just goes to show that He kept His promise."

Our neighbor had nothing to say to that. I guess he was convinced. I know I was.

The Dress Sandra Wore to the Wedding

by Ivy R. Doherty

G randma Erickson was about the most comfortable person anyone would want to have about the place. She saw a joke every time she heard one. She was always interesting to talk to. And she was always trying to make everyone happy and content.

People liked to tell her things. And I suppose that was why she was the first to hear about Aunt Laurene's wedding.

It was a balmy afternoon in early May when Grandma Erickson called Sandra into the little apartment Sandra's mother and father had fixed up for her when Grandpa passed away.

The clouds were vapor wisps that day, and the wind carried exciting perfumes from trees and grass and flowers. Grandma's dainty curtains were sailing on that same breeze when Sandra seated herself beside Grandma Erickson's rocker.

"The wind feels as though something new and wonderful is about to happen," Sandra said dreamily. "I wish whatever it is would hurry up!"

"You certainly have a good nose!" Grandma laughed. "Something exciting *is* about to happen. I have the information firsthand, and I have been given the privilege of passing it on. Seeing you are my only granddaughter, I think I'll start with you."

Grandma winked her blue eyes in the little teasing gesture she had and brushed back a stray lock of silvering hair. Then she went on rocking furiously and knitting just as fast.

"There was a letter from your Aunt Laurene in this morning's mail," she said, enjoying every word. "She is to be married on the last day of June and is coming to Wilmington for the ceremony."

Sandra's dark eyes flashed. "Wonderful!" she cried, and whirled around Grandma Erickson's rocker twice before coming to rest at the window. "Do you know who her husband will be? Is he nice?" she asked.

"I don't know," Grandma said. "But if I know Laurene, and I ought to, then I'll guess that she's marrying the handsomest, kindest young man a person could ever wish to see."

"Oh, I can't wait!" Sandra stamped her foot impatiently. "She'll be a lovely bride with her dark hair and rosy cheeks. I'll be there to try to catch her bouquet."

Grandma smiled.

"Seeing you got the news first, Grandma, it is your job to tell Mother," Sandra said. "But please hurry, because I'll burst if you wait too long."

All the time she did her piano practice, Sandra kept one ear strained for the sound of the car coming in the drive. As soon as Mother appeared, Sandra announced, "Mother, Grandma wants to see you right away."

Sandra chuckled as she thought of how soon she and her mother would be planning her dress for the wedding. Of course, there would be a new one, and weddings gave a person a chance to use her imagination. On such occasions one could wear lacy, flimsy things that looked as if they had come out of a storybook, without having the practical people say that they were impractical.

With real vigor Sandra pounced into Mother's arms when she returned from Grandma's apartment. "What are you going to wear to the wedding, Mother? What am I going to wear?"

Mrs. Erickson held up her hands. "Take it easy, dear daughter. The news is still ringing in my ears. How could I have decided already what we will wear?"

Sandra was not an easy person to put off. Within twenty-four hours it was all decided that she would wear a silky, swishy taffeta dress of lavender and lace. And within the next twenty-four hours after that just about every girlfriend Sandra had knew about the lavender dress.

Grandma Erickson got busy right away and made herself a becoming pale-blue dress, and Sandra and her mother went to town with her to choose a hat for it. Another day, when Sandra and her mother were in town, Sandra saw the very dress she had hoped for. It was so pretty! And Mrs. Erickson knew she would be very, very busy preparing for the wedding, so they decided right there in the store to buy the dress instead of making one.

With the greatest secrecy the dress was carried home and placed, still in its box, in the top of Sandra's closet.

With the same utmost secrecy Grandma Erickson purchased many skeins of beautiful pale-green silk thread and settled in her rocking chair, hour after hour, day after day, crocheting as furiously as she rocked, until at last, two weeks before the wedding, she finished what she considered to be a very handsome crocheted dress for Sandra to wear to the wedding. She wrapped it tenderly and tied it with a pale-green ribbon the same shade as the dress. She slipped in and placed the package on Sandra's bed. On the package was a pretty card that said, "With all my love, Grandma."

At bedtime Sandra made the discovery. She opened the package quickly, not knowing what to expect. She pulled out the dress and examined it with a mixture of gratitude and dismay. It was wonderful of Grandma to spend so much time on her, but where, oh, where, could she wear such a dress? It was so old-fashioned!

The girls would die laughing if they saw her in it. They would think she was up to some prank, just for fun. Grown-up people would think her mother had gone back to her childhood to imagine up such a monstrosity.

Then she saw Grandma's note pinned to the hem. It said, "For my best girl to wear at her aunt's wedding. See you the last of June."

Sandra tossed the dress on a chair and dived head-first for her pillow. What a problem. She'd never faced a dilemma like it.

She lay still for many minutes. When she was sure Grandma had gone to bed, she slipped downstairs to find her parents. She carried the dress over her arm. She handed the note she had found on the hem to her mother, who in turn handed it to Father.

The words couldn't help escaping Mother's lips: "Oh, dear!" That was all, but those two words said exactly what she felt.

"That's what I say," Sandra moaned. "Can you imagine me wearing that thing to a wedding?"

If Sandra was dismayed, Mother was equally per-turbed. She looked to Father for some ray of hope, but he had none.

"Don't worry," she told Sandra. "Let us sleep on it."

"Do you think I could sleep with a thing like this weighing on my mind?" Sandra moaned. "I won't even close my eyes all night. What about the lavender dress in my closet? Oh, surely this is a nightmare and I'll wake up in a minute. What am I going to do?"

She tried to work out a plan so that she could wear the lavender dress to the wedding without offending

Grandma. But she could think of nothing. She felt as if a horrible trick had been played on her.

The next morning she didn't feel one bit hungry and hurried over to Susan's house because she couldn't bear to face Grandma. At noon when Sandra returned, she and her mother stayed a long time in her mother's room talking about the two dresses. Mother pointed out that there was absolutely no argument about which was the prettier, the more suitable dress for the occasion.

But there was another side to the problem. Grandma Erickson's feelings had to be considered. She had made the dress lovingly, as she did everything else for the members of her family. How disappointed would she be if Sandra refused to wear the crocheted dress and turned out in the lavender and lace?

"But what would the people think?" Sandra asked.

Mother reminded her that a wedding, from the ceremony to the end of the reception, lasted, at the most, two hours. If people were surprised about the green dress, they would either understand why she had worn it, or they would soon forget it.

"But it's up to you," Mother said, "to choose the most important way to take."

Whatever else happened, Sandra decided that she must thank her grandma for the dress. That was the least she could do. And Grandma looked so happy when she thanked her that Sandra couldn't bear to think of the wedding. She realized that Grandma certainly would be disappointed if she didn't wear the crocheted dress. But, oh, dear—did she have to?

Her friends wondered why Sandra became suddenly so silent about the lavender and lace, for she had certainly talked enough about it at first.

All was hustle and bustle. Sandra threw herself into every job her mother could find for her to do. The reception was to be held in their home, and everything must be cleaned and polished. And there was so much to plan.

But there was no joy in it for Sandra. The days before the wedding were gloom and darkness and despair. She lost hope of having a magical time.

The church was packed and hushed when the Erickson family arrived, ten minutes before the ceremony. Beverly and Sharon and Linda—in fact, most of Sandra's friends—were sitting close to the aisle so they could get a perfect glimpse of the bride as she walked slowly up the aisle.

They were there for another reason too. They wanted to get a good close look at Sandra's lavender dress—the one she had spoken about so much.

Sandra knew they were there. She braced herself and marched in quickly. She looked straight ahead and tried to hide behind one of the relatives as she walked down the aisle.

It was no use. As she passed the girls, they gasped and tittered. Of course, she knew she couldn't blame them. She would have done the same if one of them had been in her place. For Sandra had decided to wear the pale-green dress. She had put Grandma's feelings before her own. She saw Beverly nudge Sharon, and she heard them whisper behind their hands as she pressed doggedly to her seat at the front.

If the bride was beautiful, Sandra never knew it. Her wretchedness was so complete that she forgot she had once looked forward to the wedding. During the reception she found many little ways to help in the kitchen with the refreshments. Then she slipped away and babysat with the tiny children who might otherwise have been in the way.

When finally the last guest was gone and Grandma was safely resting in her room, Sandra raced upstairs and pulled off the dress. She hung it in the closet and slammed the door, half hoping it would never open again. She threw herself on her bed and burst into tears.

When at last the humiliation was washed from her soul, she felt much better. There was, however, one more thorn that would surely prick her flesh in the morning. The girls would want to know about the lavender and lace. Could she hope that they'd understand? She wasn't sure if she ever wanted to see those girls again.

Her mother came in to say goodnight, and they went over the events of the wedding. At last Mother said, "The proudest moment of my day was when I saw you come out of your room in the dress your grandma made for you. You looked to me much more beautiful than any bride. Grandma will never know all you went through, but I shall always remember."

Sandra had no way of knowing that her mother let the story of the green dress leak out to the mother of one of Sandra's best friends. She was very surprised when Beverly said to her, some days later, "Sandra, I don't know how you did it, but you were really wonderful wearing that dress for your grandma's sake. I'm proud that you are my friend!"

Sarah's "Big Black Dog"

by Kay Heistand

N o, no, Sarah, you must stay home with your sister."

The little girl pouted, and tears gathered in the corners of her eyes. Sarah's mother dropped to her knees and hugged her littlest daughter.

"A mile is too far for you to walk, darling. You're only four years old."

"No! I am a big girl," Sarah insisted with a sob.

Reluctantly her mother pushed her toward their log house. Sternly she said, "Go inside with Mary and be good."

The mother and father watched the small child start toward the cabin; then they turned away. The year was 1783, and it was a lovely day in Warren, New Hampshire.

On this day Sarah's parents had an errand that would take them more than a mile away to a neighbor's house near the summit of a low mountain to the north. As they started through the woods along the trail following Berry Brook, neither of them realized that Sarah had turned around and was trying to follow them.

The little girl stayed far enough behind her parents so they could not discover her. The woods grew deeper and darker, and she found her way more difficult. Soon she could no longer hear her mother's clear laugh or her father's deep voice. Panic-stricken, she began to run. She made a wrong turn and was soon hopelessly lost in the woods.

As the light waned and night came on, Sarah grew tired. Tears claimed her, and she curled up by a big rock and cried herself to sleep.

Meanwhile, the parents visited with their friends, borrowed some supplies, and returned home just at nightfall. To their horror they discovered that Sarah was gone. Her sister had not been alarmed at her absence, for she thought Sarah was with their mother and father. Rain was beginning to fall as the frantic father alerted his neighbors, and all the townspeople started out to help him search for the lost child.

The night seemed years long to the anxious mother, who waited at home. Near dawn, the father and the other men returned. They had searched in vain all night. There was no trace of the small child, and the rain had washed away any signs of her wandering.

However, the mother did not give way to despair. Before the father could go to bed to rest or the children could eat any breakfast, the whole family knelt and prayed devoutly to God for the safety of the little girl. After the prayers the mother's heart was lightened, her faith in God renewed, and she could face the day ahead without collapsing.

From Sunday to Wednesday the search went on. Dozens of men from miles away looked day and night for at least a sign of what might have happened to the child. But no one found even a trace to show where Sarah might have gone.

Then, about noon on Thursday, a man named Heath, from the town of Plymouth twenty miles away, strode up to the cabin of the desperate parents and announced, "I know where your little girl is. Give me some food, and then I will lead you to her."

"Praise God!" cried the mother. "How do you know? Has someone found her and sent you word?" Even while the questions tumbled from her eager lips she was setting food on the table.

Sarah's father happened to be home. Haggard and hollow-eyed, he looked at the stranger skeptically. "What do you mean? Why didn't you bring Sarah home if you know where she is? I can't believe you know what you're talking about!" The father's voice was harsh, and there was no hope in his face.

But the mother's eyes were filled with hope as she listened to Mr. Heath's unusual story. "Last night I had this strange dream, not once but three times." He broke the homemade bread as he talked.

"A dream!" The father laughed roughly and came

to his feet as though to order the stranger from the cabin. "What nonsense is this?"

"Wait!" The man raised his hand, and the sincerity and honesty of his purpose shone in his plain face. His eyes were filled with memories of a vision. "Dream or vision, I know not which, but I dreamed it three times last night. Three times I saw a lost child, a little girl with light curls, about four years old—"

"That's Sarah! That's our Sarah!" the mother cried, and the tears gushed forth and down her sunken cheeks.

"Wait. I can tell you where. I found her under a big pine tree, southwest of Berry Brook, guarded by a great bear." Mr. Heath took a swallow of milk and continued. "The huge bear didn't bother me, and I didn't try to shoot it."

Now the father fell back into his chair, and his cheeks were ashen. "Some of the men found Sarah's footprints along with the tracks of a large bear, but we didn't dare tell you of this. It was too horrible to think about." He looked at his wife.

"Come now," said Mr. Heath. "We will go and find her." His calm tones carried conviction.

The father and Mr. Heath went off into the woods, heading straight for the spot Mr. Heath had seen in his dream. Hours later the waiting mother heard three gunshots from far away in the wilderness. This was to be the signal if the child was found.

Sarah's father and the man who had had the dream did indeed find Sarah asleep under a pine tree. But the dream, or vision, was incomplete, for there was no sign of a bear guarding her.

Later, when Sarah was warm and fed and rested, she was asked about her adventure. Then she told how she had awakened on the day she had first lost her way to find a "big black dog" sniffing at her scratched legs. She said she had put her arms about its neck and said her prayers. Then each evening the "big black dog" had come back and had lain down beside her to keep her warm all through each of the damp, cold nights.

The mother and father looked at each other in wonder. "The angels sent by the Lord can assume strange shapes," the mother murmured softly.

"And He sent a miraculous vision in a dream," the father answered.

4

"Five New Dresses All at Once"

by Irene Walker

But Mother," I said, "it's really hard to have to wear the same dress to school and church and everywhere else I go. You know this is the only one I have."

Mother looked troubled as she listened to my earnest words.

"Yes, dear," she said. "Your father and I wish very much that we could get you a new dress. But this is such a cold winter, and the snow has been so deep that house building is completely at a standstill, and your father has had very few days of work this winter. We'll be lucky if we don't go hungry before spring. It's a good thing you helped me can lots of fruit and vegetables from the garden. Do try not to mind too much. When spring comes we can surely get you a new dress or two."

Tears blinded my eyes as I went into my room and closed the door. I had known before talking to Mother that buying a new dress would be impossible.

"I'll just have to quit school," I muttered. "I can't go on like this. Even this dress is getting shabby and threadbare. All the other girls get a new dress once in a while."

I lay on my bed, crying softly. "Why couldn't I have been born rich?" I whispered. "Why couldn't I have been the only child in the family, like Violet down the street? With six children in our family, how could there ever be enough to go around? I'm so tired of this one old dress."

Suddenly a voice seemed to speak to me right out loud: "You could pray for a new dress. God knows how much you need one. Why don't you ask Him?"

I got up and knelt by my bed. I had learned to pray long before. But it had not occurred to me to pray about this problem.

"Dear Father in heaven," I began, "You know how very much I need a new dress. Mother and Dad can't get one for me. I have no way to earn one. Please do something to help me. Thank You, dear God. Amen."

A wonderful feeling of peace and hope came over me. Somehow I knew I could trust God to take care of me. I dried my eyes and combed my hair and went out to set the table for supper.

I could see that Mother had been crying too. When she heard me talking cheerily to the baby, she came by and patted my shoulder. "You're a brave girl," she said, and we smiled at each other.

Two or three days went by. Then one afternoon

Mother went to the nearby village. Our mail came to the post office there. She came home carrying a large package, and we all crowded around.

"What is it? Where did you get it? What's in it? Who is it from?" we all cried at once.

"I don't know what it is," Mother said. "It's from Aunt Catherine."

"Aunt Catherine," we all chorused. We had scarcely heard of her. "Open it, Mother, please."

Mother cut the string. Then to my wondering eyes she began to lift out a beautiful dress and then another. They were of lovely material, and one glance told me they were my size. There was also a coat.

"I do declare!" Mother said joyfully. "I thought Aunt Catherine had forgotten all about us. She didn't like it when we became Seventh-day Adventists, so she has never written to us or had anything to do with us since. She has a daughter just a year older than you are." Mother smiled at me. "These must be things she has outgrown. Aunt Catherine has plenty of money, so she always buys really good things. Try on one of these dresses."

I did, and the fit was perfect. My joy was too great for words.

"I wonder whatever made Aunt Catherine think of sending them," Mother said.

"God did," I answered reverently. "I prayed for one new dress, and He sent me five new dresses all at once, and a coat besides. God did it."

5

Close Call!

by Edna Craik

Dad and Everett had just finished breakfast, and they sat relaxing for a few minutes, neither one saying much. Then Dad, as was his custom, read a few verses of Scripture, and they knelt to ask God's blessing on the day.

There was nothing unusual about this particular morning. Even Mother's parting remark caused no special notice, for every morning she sent her husband and son to work with the admonition, "Be careful today, boys. Don't take any chances."

Everett stepped into the Model T Ford and started the engine. Dad climbed in beside him. It seemed that most of Everett's fifteen years had been spent at the wheel of a car or on the controls of a donkey engine or on some other piece of machinery. He loved machinery and was thoroughly at home in a car with one hand on the wheel and the other on the throttle.

The mile between home and work took father and son down a long hill, past several attractive homes, across the main highway and the railroad tracks, and through a wooded lane to the edge of the smoothly flowing Columbia River. Several hundred yards along the bank brought them to the mill.

It was a familiar route. They hardly noticed their surroundings anymore. They even had the railroad schedule memorized and lost little time worrying about the trains.

The busy morning passed quickly. About ten thirty Dad called to Everett, who was busy with a job at the water's edge. "I left some tools at home that we're needing now," he said. "Will you go home quickly and get them? They're on the back porch."

Everett left his work and drove off through the wooded lane leading to the road.

Dad and Mr. Close, the hired man, continued to work, talking now and then. Mostly, however, they were absorbed with their tasks and concentrated their attention on them.

Suddenly there was the piercing, wailing scream of a steam whistle. Mr. Close, who had worked for many years for the railroad company, dropped his tools and shouted in alarm, "Someone has been hit at the crossing!"

Both men started a dash toward the railroad crossing. The woods obscured their view, and it seemed to them that their legs had turned to soft rubber. The thought that loomed so large in their minds was

Everett was due back here just at this time. Anxiety drove them on, but fear gripped them.

When they came out of the woods, they could see the tracks. Across the tracks were scattered fenders, a hood, a car body, and various smaller parts of a car. Yes, it was the Model T Ford!

Everett had gone home, picked up the tools, and was hurrying back toward the mill. As he approached the railroad tracks, he had given the usual quick glance east, then west. Just as he decided all was clear, the morning local had rounded the bend, approaching the crossing full throttle but with no warning whistle.

Those were not the days of four-wheel brakes. At best, one did little more than chug to a stop in a methodical way. Everett applied all the brakes the little Model T afforded. With a sickening feeling at the pit of his stomach, he noted his chances but hoped and prayed for a good outcome. Then, it seemed, the danger was over.

He had managed to come to a halt at the very brink of certain death, for there were the drivers of the big engine passing by a few feet in front of his bulging eyes. He gulped and was just beginning to feel better when suddenly his world went mad.

So narrowly had he missed being on the tracks that, as the baggage coach passed, the step that extended just a few inches beyond the sides of the coach caught the bumper of the car. At this point the train had barely begun to slacken its speed. It dragged the car along the tracks and shook it to pieces.

A kindly British gentleman who lived beside the tracks had been working in his rose garden that morning and had watched the whole frightful episode. He knew the boy from seeing him pass the house every day, and his heart went down into his shoes as his mind grasped the significance of the scene before him.

Then, as the rolling, twisting car came close to him, before his unbelieving eyes out rolled its lone occupant. The wreckage passed on and left Everett lying on the ground—but only for a few seconds! For this frantic, fifteen-year-old boy started running, wild-eyed, up the tracks toward the mill.

The man who had watched it all dropped his hoe and sprang forward, catching at Everett's sleeve. "Sit down, son," he said gently. "You are all right now."

Shortly thereafter the frenzied father arrived, followed closely by Mr. Close. And then the engineer, visibly shaken, swung down from the cab of the engine. They all gave Everett a quick examination and found only two small cuts on his left leg.

As the engineer turned to go back to his post of duty, he stopped, patted Everett's shoulder, and said reverently, "My boy, there is Someone looking after you besides your mother and father."

Dad and Mr. Close agreed with a fervent "Amen."

Many years have come and gone since that fateful encounter with the steam locomotive, years during which Everett, my husband, has had many occasions to praise the heavenly Father for His never-failing protection.

6

Down the Well

by Elizabeth Montgomery

Princess! Come back here! Come here!"

Princess ignored the command.

A black border collie, the dog had been walking down an abandoned road with Cheryl Finley and Cheryl's stepsister Louvenia. All of a sudden a streak of gray and white had leaped across the path in front of her. With a series of sharp staccato barks, she had leaped into the air and headed for the woods, following hard upon her prey. She well knew what that streak was! She had chased streaks like it many times before.

On this cool, misty Sabbath afternoon, fall had already arrived in the Ouachita (Wash-i-ta) Mountains of Arkansas, near Magnet Cove. The hills were decorated with splotchy colors of red, purple, orange, henna, and yellow. But the colors this afternoon were not as bright as they might have been because the sky was overcast with clouds.

Louvenia had been making an extended visit at Cheryl's home. On this particular day the girls had gone out for an afternoon walk accompanied by the dog. Almost unconsciously they had turned their steps toward a dense grove of trees that stretched from the south edge of town toward the hills. There they had found a deserted logging road and decided to walk along it.

It was then that the streak had flashed in front of them—and Princess had disobeyed. She had always been an exceptionally obedient pet; in fact, she seldom ever refused to obey an out-and-out order.

"Oh dear!" exclaimed Cheryl as she saw her dog disappear behind some trees and bushes. "I hope she won't chase that rabbit very far."

"Oh, I'm sure she won't," Louvenia said. "Anyway, she'll know how to come back."

"I hope you're right." Cheryl furrowed her brow, trying not to worry. "But what should we do while we wait for her?"

Standing some distance back from the road was an old weather-beaten house. The windows were out and the door was open. The girls decided to explore it. Inside, they poked around the rooms, all of which proved to be uninteresting. Then they decided to go out to the old shed to see what it looked like inside. They found no attraction there either, so Louvenia suggested they start back for home.

"Not without Princess," Cheryl asserted. "I'm going down the road to see if I can call her in."

Cheryl called and called. Finally the dog showed up, but something was wrong. She was limping. Cheryl ran to meet her, and Princess came up to her, dragging her left hind foot. It had been badly cut and was bleeding profusely. Cheryl quickly removed her scarf, tore it into strips, and applied a bandage to stop the blood. She gathered the dog into her arms and started running home, with Louvenia beside her.

When she came to the old gray house, Cheryl decided to shorten the distance by cutting across the yard. As she did so, a patch of high weeds loomed up before her. She made a running jump to clear them and came down on some boards lying on the ground. The boards were rotten—and beneath them was a fifty-foot well!

Cheryl found herself falling down and down. Her head banged from one side of the rocky wall to the other. She blacked out, but came to when she struck the water. She was still holding Princess. She and the dog sank into the water, but before they touched the bottom they rose to the surface again.

It was dark down there, but feeling around, Cheryl found a ledge to grab onto. She clutched it with all her might. She drew her feet up and braced them against the opposite wall. With her hips pressed against one wall and her feet against the other, she wedged herself into a sitting position. Now the water came up to her waist. She drew Princess across her lap. All around her were old bottles, cans, pieces of boards, and other trash.

Cheryl prayed, "Jesus, help me."

In the meantime, Louvenia ran for help. Approaching the first house, she saw the owner, Mr. Coston, out near his pickup truck. "Help! Help!" she cried. "Cheryl is drowning! Back there!" She pointed to the old house.

Mr. Coston thought of the well. He jumped into his truck and tore off for the place. Mrs. Coston and Louvenia spread the alarm, and a number of men joined the rescue party.

Down in the well Cheryl's legs began to grow numb. Again she prayed, "Jesus, help me!"

Just then she looked up at the opening and saw a man's head bending over. Thinking she recognized her teacher, she asked, "Is that you, Mr. Coston?"

"Yes, Cheryl," the man answered. "We will get you out. Close your eyes. We are going to let down a ladder."

Already one or two other men had arrived. Mr. Coston needed their help lowering the ladder. This ladder was an extension ladder with a horizontal bar at the top. The men lowered it as far as the bar would let them. At this point Princess began to bark. Cheryl's legs were growing more and more numb, and every jerk of the dog's body made it harder to hold her. Cheryl quieted the dog, and the men shouted to her to climb up the ladder.

"What about my dog?" she said. "Please throw down a rope for her."

One of the men had a rope in his pickup truck. He

ran for it and dropped it down the well. Mr. Coston called, "Come up, Cheryl."

"Not without my dog," she shouted back.

Yet her legs were so numb—she knew she couldn't hold on much longer. "Jesus, help me," she prayed again, hoping that she could hold on long enough.

The rope was her only chance to save Princess. With that she must risk all! As the rope came down to her, she pressed herself extra hard against the two walls and released her handhold. With the rope she quickly made a noose and fastened it around her dog's stomach and collar. Then she lunged toward the ladder and secured the rope to the bottom rung.

"I'm ready," she called up.

Mr. Coston told her to look straight ahead and start to climb. Leaving Princess paddling in the water, she started up. Because of her numbness it was with great difficulty that she lifted her feet from one rung to another.

"Look straight ahead," Mr. Coston repeated. She obeyed.

Eager hands reached down to help her as she neared the top. When at last she was safely out, the men would have led her away at once, but she resisted them. "Not until I know Princess is safe," she said.

They pulled up the ladder and the dog came up with it, dangling from the rope at the bottom. Cheryl picked Princess up in her arms and got a grateful licking all over her face. Soon Princess's wound was taken care of, and she healed up well.

To this day Cheryl knows that God answered her prayers and performed a miracle. Several weeks before this incident Mr. Coston had seen the ladder in a store, and a strong urge had come over him to buy it. At home, his wife had asked why in the world he wanted it.

"I don't know," he had replied. "I may need it badly someday. It doesn't take up any room in the truck, so I'll just carry it around with me."

Also, Cheryl found out that the well was thirty-five feet down to the water, and the water was fifteen feet deep, well over her head. She is grateful for God's strength that helped her keep hoping for rescue and holding on until she and her dog were saved. Afterward Princess presented her with a family of eleven puppies, which Cheryl also saw as a lovely miracle.

7

Storm Baby

by Mrs. David J. Ritchie

The blizzard had set in with that unexpected suddenness that is always surprising in the foothills of western Montana. Dad had not returned from Butte, thirty miles to the north, and now, as night fell and the blizzard showed no signs of abating, it seemed obvious to us that he would remain in town until the snow stopped falling and the pass could be cleared.

My brother, Frank, lay sick with the flu. He was running a dangerously high fever, and I sponged his burning forehead with a cool cloth. Mother and Dick, the hired man, were out in the storm trying to finish the evening chores.

Presently I heard them come stomping onto the porch. A moment later the kitchen door opened, letting in a blast of icy air along with two snow-plastered figures. I went to fix them some hot Postum, and as they warmed their hands and feet, Mother and Dick talked about Old Red, one of the cows. Mother explained that Old Red had not come in at milking time. She was due to calve, and Mother and Dick were both certain she had "dropped" her calf somewhere out in the storm and refused to come in to the barn without her baby.

"We'll have to go and find her," Mother announced, starting to put on her wraps again. "The calf will freeze to death if we leave them out in this blizzard."

"Let me go with Dick," I said. "You've been out a long time already, and I haven't been out at all." I looked at Mother's frail form. I knew she had been born with a bad heart and had never been very strong.

Mother shook her head. "You are just barely over the flu yourself, Mae, and we can't risk your getting chilled and having a relapse. Has Frank's fever broken yet?"

She went into the little room off the kitchen where Frank lay. Her cool hand on Frank's hot forehead gave her the answer, and the lines of worry already deeply etched about her eyes grew deeper still. With her hand on her son's head she closed her eyes, and her lips moved in silent prayer. Watching her through the open door, Dick and I bowed our own heads and sent up silent petitions for my sick brother, and also for the lost cow and her calf.

Presently Mother left Frank's side, and once more bundled against the storm, she and Dick went out in search of the lost creatures. I filled the top of the range with kettles of water to heat for the baby calf when it would be brought in, for Mother and Dick would surely find it! Then I went to sit by Frank's bed to watch and wait.

Out in the storm in the open jeep, Mother and Dick crossed the pastures back and forth, peering into the darkness for any sign of Old Red and her calf. The wind was bitterly cold and howled so loudly that conversation was almost impossible, but it helped in one way by keeping the level ground swept clean. It piled the driven snow in drifts along the fences and in the gullies.

"Red would look for shelter," Dick yelled above the wind. "Let's look in the bushes along that draw." He pointed toward a black tangle of bushes nearby.

Mother nodded, and Dick stopped the jeep. Swinging their lanterns, the pair pushed on afoot. Suddenly Mother grabbed Dick's arm and pointed. A silhouette, darker than the bushes, materialized just ahead. Old Red!

But the work of rescue was far from finished. Somewhere in the shelter of the brush behind Old Red lay hidden a newborn calf, and the mother cow was not about to go without a battle. The storm had upset her so that she was as wild as any wild animal on the mountains. She knew only one thing—she was going to defend her little storm baby against all dangers.

She did not recognize Mother and Dick. These two familiar humans might as well have been wolves or wildcats. Old Red would not let them get near her calf.

By gestures and nods of the head, Mother and Dick worked out a plan. Dick would distract the cow while Mother crept behind her and got the calf.

Mother stood still while Dick began moving slowly around Old Red. Soon the cow determined that her greatest danger came from the moving man, and she lowered her head threateningly, turning away from Mother in order to keep him in sight. As soon as the cow was turned away, Mother darted into the brush behind her.

Yes, there was the baby, half frozen. She threw her blanket over the calf and was preparing to lift it in her arms when she heard a cry from Dick. She turned to see—but she was too late. She glimpsed fierce eyes and a lowered head, and then Old Red sent her sprawling.

Once down, there was no way for Mother to escape the angry cow's onslaughts. Old Red knelt over Mother and drove her head again and again into Mother's chest and face.

Dick yelled at the top of his voice and beat on the cow's sides until his fists were raw and bleeding, but Old Red felt nothing. Poor Mother's weak heart beat wildly. She felt herself going unconscious. She thought of how God had answered her prayer and helped them find these two lost creatures. Surely He would not forsake her now. With her last strength she cried aloud, "Oh, God, help me!"

Dick had stopped beating the cow and had started for the jeep to get the ax. Mother's cry caused him to turn. What happened next he watched through tear-dimmed eyes in stunned disbelief. For Old Red, apparently led by an unseen hand, slowly struggled to her feet and began to back away. All the time she was shaking her head as if attempting to free herself from some restraining force.

Dick ran over to Mother and lifted her in his arms. Struggling against the wind, he carried her to the jeep. Old Red seemed tethered to the ground. She watched quietly as Dick returned and picked up the calf. "Come, boss," he said to the cow, and Old Red followed obediently to the jeep and trotted along beside it all the way to the barn.

Dick took Mother and the storm baby to the house. Mother had regained consciousness and was able to walk into the house, where her swollen face and Dick's bleeding hands told their own story.

The storm baby was wrapped warmly and left close to the stove, where the heat soon revived it. Dick's hands and Mother's face were gently bathed and bandaged. It was a day or two, however, before Dick could take Mother to town, where the doctor taped her broken ribs. Hearing what had happened, he marveled that she was alive and that her injuries were comparatively slight.

"I'd like to beat that cow half to death," Frank said bitterly when he had recovered from his own illness enough to hear the story.

But Mother shook her head. "No, son. Old Red was only following her limited instincts in protecting her young. She is only a poor dumb creature, and we cannot blame her for doing what her instincts told her was right. I know God sent His angel to save my life. We can be thankful for that, and for the promise God has given of a new earth where none of His creatures will ever be driven by fear or hatred. Perhaps it would be wise for us to read Isaiah 65:25 again."

Mother opened her Bible and read aloud,

" 'The wolf and the lamb shall feed together,
the lion shall eat straw like the ox,
and dust shall be the serpent's food.
They shall not hurt nor destroy in all My holy
     mountain,'
Says the LORD."

All this happened in the winter of 1948, when I was fifteen, but I remember it as clearly as if it were yesterday. God answered Mother's prayer out there in the storm just as He had promised He would. And He will keep His promise about the new earth too. I'm hoping to be there. How about you?

8

AMY

by Goldie Down

No, this is not a story about a girl named Amy; in fact, there are no girls at all in this story. It is about a man. AMY is not a name at all in this case; it stands for After Many Years. It is a sort of code we used at our home when I was growing up; any delayed event was called an AMY. You'll see how well this title fits as my story unfolds.

Away back in 1910 Bill Jones was just an ordinary young man living in an ordinary town and working at an ordinary job. One day a colporteur came to his door and sold him a religious book.

Bill read the book and was impressed by it. It told about so many wonderful things that were in the Bible, things that Bill had not known before. Prophecies of images and dreadful-looking beasts that represented nations filled his mind. The book explained many events that had happened and many more that were going to happen.

It told about other things, too, such as what happens when a person dies, what heaven is like, and which day is God's Sabbath. It was all very interesting.

Bill had never heard of such things before, and he was pleased with his purchase. This was a wonderful book. He wondered what religion it represented. He had never heard of any church that taught these doctrines.

But Bill was not deeply religious. He believed in living by the golden rule. "Do unto others as you would have them do to you" was his motto. He would never do anyone a bad turn, and if he could do them a good one, he did it. He paid his debts and expected others to do the same. Bill didn't feel he needed any more religion than that.

Eight years rolled by, and in 1918 another colporteur came to Bill's town. The colporteur asked around for a place to stay, and people directed him to Bill's house.

"Bill's a good chap," the colporteur was advised. "He'll be sure to put you up."

So the colporteur went to Bill's house, and Bill let him stay. By day the colporteur went from house to house calling on all the people in town in an effort to sell his books. At night he sat in Bill's dining room and gave Bill Bible studies.

Once again Bill was deeply impressed by all the things he learned from the Bible. Some subjects that the colporteur studied with him Bill remembered from his own book, the one he had bought from the first colporteur. He nodded in vigorous agreement when the colporteur proved his beliefs from the Bible, but somehow the sword of the Spirit could not get through Bill's armor of self-satisfaction. It could not pierce into his heart.

"What religion are you, anyway?" he asked the colporteur. "I've never heard of anyone else but you and my book believing in these things."

"I'm a Seventh-day Adventist," replied the smiling young colporteur, "and while it is true that there are not very many of our adherents, we are advancing rapidly. This is God's great remnant church. We are getting ready to meet Jesus when He comes, and we want to help others to be ready too."

"Do you think Jesus will come in our lifetime?" Bill asked a bit skeptically.

"Oh, yes. He is coming very soon," the colporteur replied earnestly. "Why, Bill, this terrible war that has just ended [World War I, 1914-1918] is one of the signs of His coming."

"Hmm." Bill nodded. "That's true; all you say is true, but—" and once again Bill did nothing about the truths he had heard.

After the second colporteur had gone his way, Bill gradually forgot the wonderful truths he had learned. He just drifted along, an ordinary citizen in an ordinary town doing an ordinary job. He never did anything particularly bad, and he never did anything particularly good. He was a solid, respectable citizen. What more could anyone want?

Forty more years slipped quietly by. Forty-four, in fact. Bill's hair—what he had left—was gray now. His shoulders were beginning to stoop a little. He was getting perilously close to the end of his allotted span of life. Twice God had called him in his youth, but Bill had shrugged Him off.

Forty-four years had passed since the last colporteur stayed in Bill's house and taught him Bible truths, and now those truths were lost in the mists of forgetfulness.

One evening Bill was waiting at the bus stop when he saw an old friend approaching. "Joe!" he called. "Hey, Joe! I haven't seen you in years. What's the news?"

Joe crossed the street and slapped Bill heartily on the back. "The news, Bill? The biggest news is that I have just been baptized and joined the Seventh-day Adventist Church."

The mists cleared a little in Bill's mind. Somewhere a bell rang. "You have?" he questioned eagerly. "Tell me more. I used to be interested in that church a long time ago."

Briefly Joe told him more and ended by asking, "Would you like to have our pastor visit you?"

"That I would," replied old Bill heartily, "and make it soon."

The pastor visited Bill and arranged a series of Bible studies. Once more Bill heard the truths presented from the Bible, and this time, at long last, he acted upon them. Bill surrendered his life to Jesus and was baptized.

Now do you see why I called Bill's story AMY? With God, we never have to give up hope.

9

Francisco's Toothache

by Dorothy Aitken

F rancisco was the terror of the countryside. And he was clever. No matter how many crimes Francisco committed, he always managed to get around the law. No judge dared to convict him, for they knew their families would be the victims of the next wave of terror. When it came to Francisco, fear reigned supreme.

One day a shiny mission launch arrived with its captain and his wife. The announcement was made that meetings would soon be held and an onboard health clinic made available. Francisco felt that his superiority was being challenged. He let the word get around that anyone who went to the launch for treatment or who attended the meeting in the evening would be sorry.

Pedro, the launch captain, knew nothing of this, and went about getting everything ready. His wife,

Alicia, was a bit surprised when no one came to the launch to ask for medicine or treatments, but her past few weeks had been so busy that she was rather glad for the slump. She rested and wrote a few letters.

Pedro set up a small platform and ran extension cords from the boat's generator to the shore so that he could use his projector. Whistling as he worked, he was unaware of the fact that the few curious folks who showed up to watch him would never come to hear his preaching.

During the afternoon a few children gathered to watch the activity. Pedro, in his usual friendly manner, told them of the stories his wife would be sharing that evening. He whetted their appetite by mentioning the beautiful color pictures he would show them and the songs they would learn. "Hurry home and tell your parents to be sure to bring you along!" he called as they ran back into the forest.

That evening, with the meeting time approaching, Pedro ate his simple supper by the window of the launch and wondered why not one soul had shown up. Usually he had to hurry through his supper and be on hand to see that no one disconnected the projector or tinkered with the organ.

"Strange," he said to Alicia as he finished his beans and rice. "But maybe these people actually eat at the same hour as we do for a change."

Alicia smiled as she cleared the table, but by now a strange fear clutched at her heart. Suppose no one came at all. Suppose these people were superstitious and cruel. She had heard of some of the river folk who met outsiders with bows and arrows and who put poison into the water and tried to kill them in other ways. *But these people don't look like those kind of folks*, she thought.

Now it was getting dark. No one was in sight anywhere. Suddenly Pedro had an idea. "This will bring them out." He smiled as he started a small record player. "They'll hear the music and come."

But no one did. Pedro looked out into the music-flooded forest. He thought he could see shadows flitting from tree to tree. As the music blared through the darkness, Pedro walked over to Alicia. "Pray, Alicia. This could be a trick. They may be waiting for the darkness to begin their foul play, if there is to be any."

Yet somehow Pedro felt that there was to be no surprise attack. Maybe the people were more shy than the villagers upstream. Although he still couldn't be certain, he sensed that there were people hiding behind the trees and peering through the bushes.

Finally Pedro made a decision. "I am going to preach anyway," he told Alicia. "I am even going to show the pictures, just as though there were a large congregation."

Alicia played the organ, and Pedro sang energetically, praying, hoping the people would come. Then he showed the slides.

But still no one came.

The sermon Pedro preached to empty space was

powerful and convincing. He felt sure it was not falling on deaf ears, even though he could not see any listeners.

The next night was the same. And the next. And the next.

But the fifth night Pedro made an announcement. "Anyone who is ill, any who have ulcers or sores or need medical attention of any kind, can be treated. It's free," Pedro declared, looking steadily into the "eyes" of his audience, which so far as he could discern were only a cluster of tropical trees.

Daylight was just piercing the darkness when Pedro awoke the next morning. He wasn't sure what had awakened him, but he sat up in bed and looked out over the river. A few clouds in the eastern sky were turning rosy, and the parrots were beginning their morning sounds. Somewhere not far away he heard a splash on the riverbank and knew that a crocodile had slipped into the still waters. Pedro stretched and inhaled the cool morning breeze. It wouldn't be long, he knew, until the sun would come up and turn the morning's freshness into a sauna bath.

Then he heard it. It must have been what awakened him. A low moaning.

Pedro jumped out of bed. As he went past the galley window he saw the source of the sound. A man, dirty and unkempt, crouched on the riverbank, holding his hands to the side of his face.

"Ay, *hombre*," Pedro called, stepping up on deck. "What can I do for you?"

The man rose and came up on the plank that Pedro had stretched to the shore.

"It is this tooth, sir!" the man said, trembling as Pedro ran his hand over the side of his face. "It has bothered me for a long time, but two days ago it began to hurt very badly. Now my face is swollen, and I can stand the pain no longer. I heard you say last night that you were a doctor. I need help. Please, sir, won't you pull the tooth?"

"I am not a doctor," Pedro hastened to explain, "but my wife is a nurse, and she has taken a course in tropical medicine. However, I don't think she has ever pulled a tooth."

"Please, sir!" the man begged. "Try!"

"Sit here," Pedro commanded. "Tell me what your name is so I can write it on my records."

The man lowered his head. "My name is Francisco," he said softly. "You may have heard of me."

"I haven't heard *anything*," Pedro pointed out. "No one has come near enough for me to become acquainted."

Francisco grew shamefaced. "Sir, *I* am the reason no one comes to your meetings," the man confessed, brushing his bushy moustache thoughtfully. "I am the terror of this country, and I threatened anyone who came near your launch." He sat down on the chair Pedro offered. "But if you will pull this tooth, I promise to change all that."

Pedro paused, then said, "We shall try."

Turning, Pedro headed down to the living quarters of the boat and awakened Alicia. "You must come and pull a tooth, dear. Where are those old forceps we used to have?"

"I don't know—I never used them. And I don't know how to pull a tooth!" The woman tumbled out of bed, muttering about the early hour.

"Well, you've got to use them this time. You'll have better success than I will. This man has a terrible toothache, and he is the key to our having an audience tonight."

Alicia fumbled around in some drawers and finally came up with several forceps. "I don't know a thing about them," she said. "They were with the medical supplies when we took over the boat. I don't know which is for the top or the bottom! Pedro, *you* do it. I'll come up and give the injection, though I must admit I don't know exactly where to give it!"

While Alicia dressed, Pedro found the syringe and the anesthetic they used for minor wounds. The twosome headed back to the clinic area, where Pedro sterilized the forceps as best he could and arranged his meager tools on a sterile bandage. Alicia administered the anesthetic to Francisco, still not sure she was doing it right. Finally she handed the forceps to Pedro.

Up to this moment Pedro had thought the morning was delightful. Suddenly he was sweating a cold, clammy perspiration, and his hands were shaking. "I'm no dentist," he whispered.

"Neither am I," retorted Alicia. "But I've seen a tooth extracted. Just get hold of the tooth and pull . . . I guess."

"Francisco, open your mouth wide," Pedro instructed. After a few tries, Pedro got a firm grip on the aching tooth. He pulled and pulled, and finally the tooth began to budge. Then the forceps slipped. Pedro looked at his patient sitting there so calmly, his countenance emitting confidence and trust.

"Don't mind me," Francisco said when he saw the beads of perspiration running down Pedro's face. "I can take it. You just get that tooth out of there."

After much effort, the tooth finally slipped out. Alicia stuffed sterile gauze into Francisco's mouth, and they sent him on his way. Francisco went down the gangplank muttering through the gauze, "You'll have a crowd tonight."

And that night they did! And Francisco, the *former* terror of the countryside, was the first person to accept Jesus as his Savior.

10

Joe's New Belt

by William S. Johnson

You can trust this belt, Joe. It's brand-new. You needn't worry, no matter how high you are—not with this new belt to support you."

The foreman of the electric supply gang handed over the belt. It was no ordinary belt; it was thick and strong and several inches wide, and it was locked by a heavy, shiny brass buckle.

"Thanks, boss," Joe said. "Sure is a fine belt."

He looked up at the wooden pole and noticed that it reached far above the high-tension wires. Then he looked down at the belt again. That belt would have to carry the weight of his body as he worked high above the wires.

Joe Miller was rather new to this kind of work, but he liked it and had already won the favor of the foreman of the gang that erected poles and strung new power lines in the state of New South Wales, Australia.

For Joe, the job had come as a welcome relief. He and his wife had joined the Seventh-day Adventist Church a short while ago—and Joe had been fired from his last job as a result. He had decided to honor God even if it did mean being out of work. But what made the decision especially difficult was that these were the days of the Great Depression, and all over the world jobs were very scarce.

For some months after his baptism Joe had been without work. He and his wife and the two boys had to make do in a little old run-down, two-roomed hut. Every evening the family had gone down to the nearby seacoast, and Joe had scooped out two hollows in the soft sand. His wife had wrapped the boys in thick blankets and laid them in the hollows to sleep. Then Joe and his wife had climbed out on the rocks and spent the night fishing. They had done that night after night (except Friday night) for months.

You can see that life had been hard for the new Adventist family—but God had not forgotten them. After a while Joe had found this job with the electric supply gang, and now on this bright crisp morning, when the kookaburras were laughing at the world from the gum trees, the boss had selected Joe for a special assignment.

"Look, Joe," he had said, "I've got a very tricky job for you today. You see that new pole over there? Somehow there was a mistake about the measurements, and it's about six feet higher than the others. I want you to climb up and saw off the top six feet. And for this special job, you can have a new belt!"

Joe looked at the belt again. It would have to give him good support. When he reached the top of the pole he would buckle the belt around the pole and lean back to saw the pole. If the belt broke . . . but why worry? These belts never broke; and besides, this was a new one!

Joe picked up his saw and several of the metal spikes the men used for climbing poles. The poles had holes drilled at regular intervals, and as Joe climbed he inserted the spikes in the holes to form a sort of ladder.

Up he went, clear to the level of the high-voltage wires, then through them and above. The words of his boss were going through his mind as he climbed. As he placed a spike and set his foot on it, he would say to himself, "Trust in the belt." Then with the next step he would say, "Trust in the Lord."

And so, trusting in the belt as he came down on his left foot and trusting in the Lord on his right, he reached the top of the pole. He set his feet firmly on spikes on both sides of the pole and took out the belt. He put it around the pole and snapped the big buckle. Then he gradually leaned out from the pole until his body was supported only by the metal footrests and the belt. Slowly he began to saw off the top six feet of the pole.

Far down below, the foreman gazed up at Joe. He was so interested in what was happening up there that he didn't notice the arrival of the inspector (who had the habit of showing up unexpectedly) until the inspector said, "Who's that on the pole?"

The foreman turned to find the inspector. "Oh, that's Joe Miller," he said. "He's fairly new, but he's a good worker. Doesn't drink. Besides, he has a new belt."

"I suppose you turned off the electricity?" the inspector said.

The foreman's face fell. "Well, no, I didn't. This is only a quick job, and, anyway, Joe's a very reliable fellow."

The inspector spoke again, more sharply. "You know the government regulations about this. Maybe you should get that power turned off right away."

The foreman knew better than to argue. He hurried down the road to the circuit box some five hundred yards away, inserted the key, and switched off the power. He was rather crestfallen as he turned to make his way back to the pole. Somehow the inspector always came at the wrong time!

The rasping of Joe's saw still rang out through the crisp morning air. The foreman looked up—and froze with horror! For Joe was falling. The new belt had broken!

And then suddenly Joe stopped falling. He jerked to a halt, suspended by one arm from a high-tension wire. What had happened? As Joe was sawing into the pole, the belt had broken, suddenly leaving Joe to plunge to his death. A split second later Joe had felt something hit his side. It was a wire; and as fast as though he had pulled his arm close to his body, he had latched onto the wire. Now he hung up there, swaying on the wire that was hooked under his armpit.

Other workers in the gang quickly brought a ladder on wheels, and moments later Joe was safely on the ground again.

Everyone crowded around to inspect the belt. The big brass buckle on the belt had snapped in two!

But God had saved Joe's life; He had saved him from death by falling and from death by electrocution.

Joe continued to work on the lines. He still climbed tall poles. He still used the lineman's belt. But each time, as he climbed a pole, he no longer said "Trust in the belt—trust in the Lord." Now it was "Trust in the Lord" on every step. And the words of the Bible meant more and more to him: "Trust ye in the LORD for ever: for in the LORD JEHOVAH is everlasting strength" (Isaiah 26:4, KJV).

Underwater Miracle

by Arlene Potter

O ne, two, three, heave!" I directed as three of my best friends, clad in swimsuits and cutoffs, jerked the huge container of ice-cold lemonade onto the station wagon tailgate. We were eager to finish loading and be on our way.

"The sun is really hot today. If you don't get me to that river fast, I think I'll die of heatstroke," threatened Sally.

"Don't worry," I consoled with mock concern. "If you don't make it there alive, we'll tie you to an inner tube and let you float along with us anyway."

"Before anyone dies, let me collect all the permission slips," laughed Mr. Green, our faculty sponsor, his arms adorned with large black inner tubes.

Seven wrinkled slips of paper with the required parents' signatures emerged from pockets, wallets, and purses. Mr. Green counted them. "Who didn't bring one?"

"Uh . . . er . . . me, sir. Remember, you said I could just phone my mom and ask her, since she lives in town?" I stammered, hoping that would end the conversation.

"That's right. So you did call her, didn't you?"

"Yes, sir, she said it was all right," I lied, my face reddening. But to my relief, Mr. Green didn't seem to notice.

A few weeks before, when we'd planned the inner-tube expedition down the Verde River, he'd explained that some of the rapids were a bit hard to handle. He said he didn't want to take any academy dormitory students unless they had permission from their parents. That night I'd called my mom and told her about the plan just to test her reaction to the idea.

"Well, I think it's dangerous. Someone drowned out there last summer. Anyway, I'm glad you're not going," she had said finally. After that I'd been afraid to bring the subject up.

Oh, well, I wasn't getting myself into any real danger. Besides, when I got back all safe and sound, Mom would be glad I'd gone and had a good time.

We all helped load potato chips, fresh fruit, and a luscious-looking chocolate cake into the two waiting cars. After tying the inner tubes on top, we bowed our heads for a word of prayer, which served only to make me more uncomfortable.

As soon as the station wagon rolled onto the highway, we all burst lustily into our school song. The car door windows almost rattled out as we got louder and louder toward the ending: "From the east, to the west, To us you're the best, Thunderbird A-cad-e-my!"

With that song over, one of the girls started another: "Nothing Between My Soul and the Savior."

Why couldn't she sing something more lively? I thought as the others joined in. Besides, the words stabbed at my conscience.

Guilty feelings all but vanished, though, when the beautiful grass-banked Verde came into view. Soon we were floating lazily downstream, soaking up the hot Arizona sun and watching the scenery go by. Overhead, puffy white clouds dotted the azure sky.

This is the life, I thought, shutting my eyes and letting my head rest on the back of the inner tube. *I sure am glad I came. What Mr. Green and Mom don't know won't hurt them. And besides, none of this seems one bit dangerous!*

After about an hour of leisure floating, we came to the first rapids. The white foam leaped between the protruding rocks furiously. But with deft maneuvering and quick paddling, we all made it through without any mishaps. It felt exhilarating to be swishing along at such a rate with water spraying coolness on our sunburned cheeks.

"Whee! That was fun! Did you guys see how fast I was going?" I exclaimed excitedly.

However, after the next rapids I wasn't quite so

enthusiastic. I had not detected some of the rocks hiding under a few inches of water and had encountered several of them rather abruptly through the opening of my inner tube.

"What's that loud roaring noise?" I called to the others ahead of me moments later.

"That," shouted Mr. Green, knowingly, "is the river's way of warning us of the bigger rapids just ahead. Here's where the fun begins! Be sure you hang on to your inner tubes and you'll be OK."

The other girls grinned in eager anticipation, but since I wasn't exactly an expert at this sport, judging from my numerous bruises already, I decided I'd better get out and walk along the edge. These were the rapids where novice floaters occasionally got banged up and a few had even lost their lives.

But somehow I had misjudged the swiftness of the already too-strong current. Frantically I began paddling toward the bank. "Help! Somebody get me out of here! I don't want to try these rapids!" I screeched, but the deafening roar of crashing water drowned out my cries. The only thing left to do was to follow the others and hope for the best. After all, if they could make it, why couldn't I?

The first part of the rapids consisted of a huge jagged rock jutting up in the middle of the river with two relatively small waterfalls on each side, one more dangerous than the other. Mr. Green and a few of the girls headed for the more difficult one, while the rest aimed for the other. Naturally I wanted to take the easier way, but somehow my inner tube caught the wrong current, and all of a sudden I found myself behind Mr. Green, being swept toward the more formidable falls. My hands dug into the water like two steam shovels going full force as I tried desperately to change my course. That was the wrong thing to do, I soon discovered, for now I was rushing directly toward the monstrous, jagged rock in the middle of the river.

In an effort to avoid a painful collision, as soon as I came into its range I kicked the rock with one foot as hard as I could—another mistake, I discovered. The jolt threw me off my inner tube and against the rock, making a painful gash in my arm. Then the swirling water shoved me under one of the waterfalls.

Water gushed into my nose and mouth before I got a chance to close them. Choking and gasping as water went down the wrong pipes, I immediately tried to surface for air, but the pressure of the crashing water pounded me down to the riverbed. Crouching low, I made a powerful lunge for the surface, but to no avail. Again and again I tried, but the weight of the water overpowered my efforts. My lungs ached and my head was spinning. A beautiful blue sky and fresh, life-giving air were but a few feet from me, but I was powerless to reach them.

The awful realization that I was only a moment away from death struck me. *I'll pray*, I thought.

Suddenly my mind flashed back to the words of the song I had heard a few hours before: "Nothing between my soul and the Savior . . . Nothing between,

. . . let nothing between." The full impact of the song hit me. There was definitely something between. Was that one little lie going to cause me to die without hope? Would it be my last recorded deed? I felt feverish. If people could perspire underwater, I would have.

"Oh, God," I prayed, "forgive me. Don't let me die with that sin between us. Please."

At once my burden was lifted, and I knew that God had forgiven me. New hope surged through my veins. I gathered up what little strength I had for what I felt would be my last try. I crouched low for the jump, but my legs suddenly felt like jelly, and my whole body started to collapse. *It's no use*, I thought.

Nevertheless, forcing myself, I made that last feeble attempt. At that instant, an angel must have bent to help, for, miraculously, I felt myself being scooped out from under the thundering falls. Defying all of nature's water laws, up, up, to that beautiful blue sky and wonderful air I was lifted. Gratefully, I swallowed a huge gulp of air. I realized that God had intervened.

Then I was under again, but this time instead of being held under the waterfall, I was propelled through the rest of the rapids. My leg slammed against a rock. My head banged another one. I felt like a Ping-Pong ball being paddled back and forth. But I no longer had any fear.

Finally the current slowed down. And just when I thought perhaps I could stand up, I felt myself being lifted out of the water by my friends. Their ashen faces showed their concern as they helped me. But I was no longer afraid. God—my hope—had saved me, and I determined to keep nothing between us.

12

I Dare You!

by Thirza M. Lee

When my brother Nat started daring me last Friday, I didn't know that I was heading for big adventure. We don't go in for daring each other much at our house; Mom and Dad sort of discourage it. But there was nothing to do Friday afternoon—it was just too hot!

Suddenly from the blanket he had spread on the back lawn, Nat drawled sleepily, "Dare you to jump across the fish pool."

As I said, our folks really discourage this type of thing, but I didn't mind about a little thing like jumping the fish pool. When I landed triumphantly on the other side, just barely missing Mom's special Japanese irises, I grinned wickedly at Nat.

"Aw, sis," he wailed, "I was all set to hear a splash! Dare you to walk the porch rail."

"But Mom said if I do it one more time—" I began.

Nat interrupted in a mocking whisper, "Mom said, Mom said . . . I know what she said. But I also happen to know that at this moment she's sound asleep in her hammock on the patio!"

And that was how I came to have my big adventure—not a pleasant adventure, but quite educational. Mom always says I get into these mix-ups because I don't stop to think. And Dad says a head was wasted on me because I never seem to use it.

So when Nat eventually dared me to ride old Mike alone up the back side of Badger Mountain, I didn't stop to think if it was sensible or not. I just yelled "Hah" defiantly and tore off to the barn. All I took with me was my cowboy hat—my sombrero, I called it—because a girl needs a proper hat for riding, even if the horse is an old nag like Mike.

I don't think either Nat or I ever really understood why we were absolutely forbidden to ride on the far side of Badger Mountain. Dad always talked about the dangers—all that loose rock and shale from the slides and the fact that there were no trails or fences or definite landmarks to keep us from getting lost. But we never took his warnings too seriously. I guess teenagers are like that sometimes; we have to bang our heads against a rock wall before we believe it's there. I did understand, though, about some other rules I was breaking—like going off alone without telling the folks where I was going.

As it turned out, there was nothing so tough or terrifying about riding up Badger Mountain. I didn't see any snakes, and old Mike didn't stumble on the shale or cause a landslide. And all the time I had a clear picture in my head of the way I had come and how to find my way back.

The only trouble was that I was hot and dry and thirsty—just as I had been on the lawn at home, only more so. There was nothing to make me afraid or even make me feel guilty about what I was doing. Dad says sometimes Satan tricks us like that; Satan makes us think we're being awfully smart when really we're just acting like plain old-fashioned fools.

So I was riding along, singing a rousing song, when in a flash it happened. A little brown rabbit jumped from a clump of sagebrush and went hopping out right under old Mike's nose! He snorted in surprise and jumped higher than he had jumped for many years. I flew through the air and landed abruptly and painfully on a heap of jagged shale. Suddenly everything was chaos and blinding pain.

For what seemed a long time I didn't think at all (Mom would have said it was too late to start anyway!). I was simply enveloped in pain and shock and surprise. Then I began to realize vaguely that Mike had gone and I was alone—and that somewhere I hurt as I had never hurt before.

Where was I hurt? I tried to corral my senses and take stock. My leg was surely the source of that terrible grinding pain! I was sprawled facedown, sort of hanging over the pile of rocks. Every time I tried to move, sharp knives darted up my leg.

My cheek and both arms were cut, too, but these were smaller hurts, the kind I could take hold of and manage. But the pain in my leg was much bigger than anything I could handle. I kept wiggling and turning as much as I could, and at last I caught sight of my other half—those long legs that so often led me into trouble.

I could see at a glance that my right leg was broken. It was swollen and purplish, with a sharp hump on one side that I knew must be the end of a bone. My head swam dizzily again, and I felt sick and absolutely terrified! Then, suddenly, all the things that I should have thought about before began pounding into my head.

I realized I was utterly alone and very far from home. Nobody knew where I was—well, Nat more or less knew, of course, but he wouldn't tell for fear of incriminating himself. Mom and Dad wouldn't even know I was in trouble until nighttime! I was badly hurt and lying unprotected underneath a blazing sun. I was in trouble, and I knew it.

Never before had I felt so terrifyingly alone and completely helpless. I wasn't used to feeling helpless, for I always considered myself pretty capable of managing on my own. That was one reason I had never been too keen on religion. When you're fourteen and pretty smart, who needs any help from God?

So here I was, alone and bashed on the rocks on the far side of Badger Mountain. I suppose, according to my folks, God was out there somewhere, too, but I couldn't quite see how it was going to help me any. I wanted to think that if God was as good and kind as my parents said He was, then He wouldn't have let me get into this fix anyway. But I knew a good deal better than that!

So finally I began to do some straight thinking. I knew I had only myself to blame for the mess I was in. If only I had some water and some shade! Suddenly I spied my hat perched jauntily, almost teasingly, on top of a small rock nearby.

Could I reach it? Well, I could try! I reached and stretched with all my might—I'm sure I grew an inch—but it was still tormentingly just beyond my fingertips. Finally I speared it with a sharp stick. With my wide hat covering my head and neck, I felt a little better. Not much better, though.

I was thinking and puzzling as hard as I could in between groaning and the awful pain, feeling wretched from the heat and dryness. And then somehow I was doing more than thinking. God had taken a hand in the situation, and I knew I was praying! I didn't even think I believed in praying, or in God, for that matter, and here I was really praying! And you know, it wasn't hard at all, and it didn't make me feel like a sissy or anything. It was sort of like talking over my problems—my weaknesses, I guess—with Mom and Dad when they're being real understanding, or with the school counselor. And I started to feel a lot better—inside, I mean; the outside parts of me were still pretty sore.

Maybe it was because I was seeing things a little clearer, or maybe it was because I sort of had God on my team now. Anyway, I could see a small ray of hope. Just a few feet in front of me was a huge rock shoulder that stood out like a shelf. Beneath it there was an inviting, cool-looking patch of black shade.

There I had to drag myself, I knew. Crawling those few short feet was the hardest thing I had ever tried. Every little move I made started more jabbing pains in my smashed leg, and I kind of passed out with each short drag I made; but it was getting me closer to that shade.

I don't even remember crawling the last few inches or pulling myself under the rocky overhang. But I must have done it before I passed out completely, because that's where Dad and Nat found me just before dark. Old Mike to the rescue, wouldn't you know! He had strolled home in his thoughtful way without me, and Nat, being fairly bright for a boy, knew at once that I must have been ditched somewhere out on Badger Mountain.

I guess Nat's conscience pricked him pretty hard for a while. He seemed to feel worse than I did, because he thought it was mostly his fault. Anyway, he kept telling me how they brought me home, how they made a stretcher out of two small trees and their jackets, and how he came home for a flashlight because it got too dark to see their way down off the mountain.

It must have been exciting, just like the stuff you read in books. And to think I missed all the fun! But if I'd been conscious, I probably would have screeched every time they moved me! Maybe that's an example of

Dad's pet saying: "All things work together for good if we trust God."

My dad and mom have a whole host of these "helpful sayings" that they shoot at Nat and me to help keep us going straight. Anyway, I'm going to have a lot of free time for thinking for a long time to come.

All of this stuff I'm writing from my bed in the hospital. Nat fixed up a snazzy bed-desk for me so I can write and read. I have to lie flat on my back for what seems like forever. My poor banged-up leg is in traction to pull it back into shape again.

The doctor tells me I'll be as good as new in a few months. A few months! It seems to me a kid can do a lot of thinking—and likely a lot of praying, too—in a few months! I'm sure glad I learned how.

13

Babysitter for a Coon

by Lois Mae Cuhel

Keven Mattson was collecting wood for the camp stove when he heard a whir of propeller blades. He looked down the channel that ran behind their cabin in Itasca State Park. He saw his father bring in their pontoon—a shallow boat with a propeller mounted on the rear.

Keven hurried to the landing and fastened the boat with ropes. As he helped unload some supplies, he noticed a small black ball of fur on some rags in the hold. It shone in the brilliant morning sunlight.

"It's a baby raccoon," Dad said. "I spotted it in the woods along the bank of the waterway."

Keven had lived in the north woods of Minnesota all his years, but he had never seen a baby raccoon before. It looked like a house cat, except for its pointed nose and large tail. It opened its eyes, then looked about and made a soft whimpering sound.

"How did you ever get it away from its mother?"

"The mother was nowhere around. I couldn't leave it to starve, so I brought it in with me. Cute little fella, isn't it?"

Keven ran ahead of his father to the house. "Mom, come look! Dad brought us a baby raccoon."

Keven's mother came to the screen door. "Why," she said, "it looks just like a pretty little kitten. The poor thing must be hungry. I'm going to warm some milk for it."

Mrs. Mattson went into the kitchen and soon came back with a small dish of milk, which she put near the baby raccoon. It didn't move. Keven dipped his fingers into the milk and drew them gently over the animal's lips. The baby raccoon licked its lips.

"It's just a baby," Mrs. Mattson laughed. "We should get a bottle."

"That's a real problem," said Keven's father. "We haven't had a baby's bottle around the house for years."

"Then we'll have to make our own bottle," Mom announced. "Let's see what we can find around the house."

Mrs. Mattson found a bottle and told Keven where to get an old rubber glove. They filled the bottle with warm milk and fastened a finger of the glove to the top, then cut a small hole in the end of the finger.

Keven took the bottle and put the finger in the baby raccoon's mouth. The baby knew exactly what to do. It drank the milk and then settled down and fell asleep.

Keven stroked its fur. "You surely are sleek," he said. "I just know your mother took good care of you."

"What about its mother?" Mom asked. "Where is she?"

"She must be hurt somewhere in the forest," Dad answered. "No wild mother ever leaves her baby for long if she can help it. This baby raccoon must have been left for a couple of days."

Keven made a bed from a box with high sides. He lined the bottom with the softest rags he could find. Then he lifted the sleeping raccoon and gently put it in the box.

That night Keven lay on his bed and stared at the creature in the moonlight. He couldn't go to sleep for a long, long time.

The raccoon grew stronger day by day. It began to follow Keven all around the camp. He called it Pokey.

One morning before breakfast Keven walked down to the channel with Pokey trotting behind him. He sat on the bank to watch the forest wildlife stir in the early morning light. Loons and cranes flew over the tall grass and landed in the water. Hundreds of frogs croaked, and the birds sang. Keven loved the aroma of pine needles on the damp, cool forest air. The Itasca State Park forest was wide awake.

Pokey playfully nipped Keven's toes, and Keven scolded the raccoon with a light tap on its nose. "Don't bite, Pokey," he said.

A soft, rustling sound made Keven glance up the bank. About ten yards away he saw a large raccoon in a clearing. It had come so quietly that he had not heard it. It stood still and watched the boy and the baby raccoon. Keven remained motionless.

"Keven, Keven," called his father, "come in for breakfast."

Keven was afraid to turn his head. "Look down the bank, Dad," he said quietly. "I think it's the mother raccoon."

"Don't move, son."

Keven waited motionless as the larger raccoon crept closer. Pokey didn't see it and continued to play with Keven's toes.

The raccoon headed straight for the baby. A fly crawled across Keven's face, but he didn't even twitch his nose. He knew he must not move.

The raccoon sniffed and sniffed. For a moment or two it acted as if it were going to walk off again, but it began to lick the baby's fur. Pokey rubbed happily against her. Then the mother turned around and headed for the underbrush, confident that her baby would follow her. It did.

Keven's father came up behind him and put his hand on his son's shoulder. "It's better this way," he said in an understanding voice.

"I'm going to miss Pokey," said Keven, not a bit ashamed of a couple of tears that were sliding down his cheeks.

"It would have happened sooner or later," said his father. "Even if the mother hadn't come, we would have had to turn Pokey loose in the Itasca forest when he was grown. But," he added, "someday you might see him again."

Keven hoped that would be so, and he knew just how it could happen. He would be rowing down a quiet channel of the lake when he would see Pokey, a full-grown raccoon with black markings on his face like the mask of a bandit. Keven would recognize the ringed tail and lumbering gait. Pokey would look straight at him with his bright eyes and remember. And they would always be neighbors, part of the beautiful wild world of the forest.

14

Multiple Miracle

by Liz Sweeney

B ye!" The words rang out in the clear night air and followed the station wagon across the silent campus.

Mrs. Grant turned the car toward the exit, and everyone inside settled back for a long ride home.

"Wish we could have seen the end of the basketball game," said Dawn, curling up in the back part of the wagon and pillowing her head on her arms.

"Right," agreed Suzanne. "But it was great to see Sis anyway and go to the junior-senior benefit program. It was really good."

In the front seat beside Suzanne, Gordon Chambers sat wide-awake but lost in thought. He was remembering the good time he had had with his brother that day. It had been nice, he reflected, to have Mrs. Grant take him along with her two daughters on their trip to East Ridge Academy.

A gentle rain spattered the windshield as Mrs. Grant piloted the car along in the darkness. Occasionally there would be a "splat" as the car hit a puddle. But inside there was a sleepy silence.

After a while Mrs. Grant spoke. "Gordon, would you mind taking the wheel for a while? I'm getting awfully sleepy." She rubbed one eye with the back of her hand.

"Sure, Mrs. Grant, be glad to." Gordon sat up straighter and prepared to exchange places with her. Soon he was behind the wheel, Mrs. Grant was in the middle, and Suzanne was settled next to the door.

"Gordon, just one request," said Mrs. Grant as they pulled away from the shoulder. "It's pretty slippery, and every time we hit a puddle it seems to pull the car to the right. So please keep the speed down to forty-five miles per hour."

Gordon nodded assent, and on they went into the blackness. As he drove he noticed that the roads worsened and the shoulder became nonexistent. But he wasn't worried—he'd driven in worse weather and on a lot worse roads.

Then it happened! The car swerved off the road, its right wheels dropping down off the pavement. Gordon fought desperately, but it was no use. The mud along the highway's edge was slippery, and the harder he tried to turn the car back onto the highway, the more they slid.

Gordon's mind reeled. He tried to step on the brake, but the pedal seemed to be moving away from him. Then an unknown mass loomed in front of them.

"Oh!" they all exclaimed as they just missed it and sailed through the air. They were to learn later that they were airborne for twenty feet and that the ditch into which they slid was thirty feet deep. There was a sickening thud as the car landed.

For a few seconds, shock held them all in its grip. Then Gordon looked around him. "How in the world did I get back here with you?" he asked Dawn as he saw that he was in the rear of the station wagon.

She sat up, befuddled with sleep. "Search me! What I'd like to know is, How did we get upside down?"

Gordon gave a start. It was true. They were sitting on the inside of the roof of the car. He looked up. Mrs. Grant was at the front of the car with Suzanne. Blood was running down her face from a cut above her eye.

"Are you two all right?" she asked in a dazed way. "Suzanne seems to be OK."

"We're OK too," Gordon assured her.

"What do we do now?" asked Dawn.

"Well, I'd say the smart thing to do would be to get out of this car," said Mrs. Grant. "Hear the water rushing around us? We're upside down in water."

Dawn shoved open a side door a crack, only to have water come pouring in. She struggled to close the door.

"Oh, no, Dawn, don't shut that door!" exclaimed Mrs. Grant. "It's our only way out. These doors up front won't open at all."

Gordon scooted over to the door and vented every ounce of his energy against the angry currents outside that threatened to seal them in the car. He finally managed to force the door open and shove Dawn out. The water tugged at her with strong arms.

"Hang on, Dawn," yelled Gordon frantically. "Hang on to the door handle."

Dawn hung on with all her might while she worked her way around the front of the car to safety. Behind her, Gordon reached out to help Mrs. Grant and Suzanne who were struggling to get out of the car.

"Hurry, Suzanne!" ordered her mother. "The car's filling with water—and fast."

Several frantic moments followed as the three made their escape from the car and clawed their way up the bank.

"Car lights!" exclaimed Mrs. Grant. "Quick, kids, get up the bank and flag that car down!"

Gordon was suddenly aware that they had met very few cars that evening and that this might be their last chance to get help. Fear lent speed to his legs and arms. He reached the edge of the highway just as the car approached, its headlights shining brightly through the darkness.

"Stop! Stop!" The group waved their arms in wide circles as the car bore down upon them. And, joy of joys, the car slowed down and stopped.

It was a strange sight that met the gaze of the driver as he climbed from his car. Four muddy figures stood beside the road—two young girls, wet and bedraggled;

a shivering boy; and a shoeless woman with blood still trickling down her face.

Gordon squinted back at their rescuer through blurry eyes. His glasses had been lost.

On the way to town the whole story came out. The stranger gasped as he realized the full impact of the accident through which the group had just passed. So did the sheriff when he was told about it.

"Folks," he said, "I've got to take the driver back to the scene to fill in the details."

Gordon wearily plodded after the sheriff while the rest of the group were provided with warm blankets.

"Thank you so much," said Mrs. Grant. "We had our coats off in the car because of the heater, and I guess they were swept away."

"Where are your purse and glasses, Mom?" asked Dawn worriedly.

Her mother frowned. "They got lost too," she admitted ruefully.

"With your paycheck and everything?" cried Suzanne.

"I'm afraid so, dear."

Soon Gordon and the sheriff returned. The sheriff was shaking his head. "You're mighty lucky, ma'am," he said in wonderment. "You should all still be in that car!"

The next day the group returned to the scene of the accident and stared at their ruined car.

"If we had landed just a few feet closer to the highway, we would have been in water at least twenty feet deep," murmured Mrs. Grant.

"And we just missed that huge rock pile," shivered Dawn. "Think what might have happened to us on that!"

Mrs. Grant was inside the car, rummaging through the mud. "My glasses," she said, her eyes shining. "And my purse!" She dug through it rapidly. "Everything's here—and there's no water damage!"

"Look! Even our coats." Suzanne held them up.

"But they're ruined." Mrs. Grant gave her verdict as she surveyed the mud-coated objects. "They'll never look nice again."

Several days later Mrs. Grant finished washing and drying the coats. "I can't believe it, girls," she exclaimed. "They're as good as new."

Everyone stared with disbelief. But it was true. Even Dawn's white-trimmed coat looked as beautiful as it had the day she bought it.

"God certainly performed a miracle for us," stated Dawn firmly.

"Not just one miracle, dear," said her mother thoughtfully. "Many small ones—everything from saving our lives to helping the trim on your winter coat come clean." And they were all silent, pondering again God's wonderful love and care for His children.

15

Don't Jump!

by Peggy Hodges

H ey, Greg, I finished my driver's training, and I can go down and get my license today. I just called to see if the license examiner is in, and he is."

Greg smiled at his younger friend. He knew what Dave wanted but decided to let him struggle on. Anyone who had enough nerve to borrow a car should have enough nerve to ask for it, he figured.

"The only thing is—" Dave squirmed. "My dad is gone for a week, and my sister says no way am I going to drive her brand-new Mustang. So I thought . . ."

Greg waited patiently.

Dave looked at his friend and decided Greg wasn't going to offer the car. So he plunged in. "I thought maybe I could use your car to take the test."

Greg laughed. "Yes, you may use the car! Why didn't you just up and ask instead of taking so long?"

"I was afraid you'd say no, and I want to get my

license as soon as possible. I just know Dad will let me use his old pickup when I can legally drive. Can we go now?"

"Come on," Greg said. "I'll drive you over to the office, and when you get your license you can drive me back home."

"Wow," Dave bubbled over as he fastened his seat belt, "what I wouldn't give for a car like this!"

"All you have to do is save your money for years and years, and you can have one too."

"Let's go across the Broadway Bridge," Dave suggested. "I've never been that way."

Greg quickly agreed. The traffic was light, and it was always interesting to cross the high silver span with its commanding view of the beautiful river below. As they started across they watched a group of sailboats that were traveling together.

"That looks great," Dave remarked. "I've always wanted to go on a sailboat."

He leaned out to get a better look at the glistening white sails, and then yelled suddenly, "Stop the car!"

"Forget it!" Greg retorted, pointing to the no-parking signs on the bridge posts.

"You have to!" Dave caught his arm. "A woman just crawled over the railing. She's probably going to commit suicide. We've got to stop her!"

Greg pulled over close to the pedestrian walk and stopped the car. "You and your imagination! I don't see anyone."

"Right there!" Dave yelled over his shoulder as he

ran toward the center of the span. He grabbed frantically at the young woman's arm.

She was clinging to the railing and looking at the deep, calm river below.

"Don't touch me!" she yelled wildly. "I'm going to jump, and you can't stop me!"

Greg, who was close behind Dave by now, sized up the situation quickly. The woman appeared to be in her twenties. She was dressed in jeans and a striped top. Her hair blew wildly about her face, and her dark eyes were all pupil as she struck at Dave.

"Probably high as a kite on dope," Greg muttered.

He knew that if Dave wasn't careful, she could easily pull him over the railing and into the river with her. He had to give Dave credit for thinking only of the woman's safety.

"Leave her alone, Dave," he advised. "I don't think she'll jump."

"I'll jump!" screamed the woman. "Take your hands off me! I want to see the Lord. I must talk to Him. He won't listen to me down here, but He will when I see Him."

A large truck pulled up behind Greg's car. The driver came running over. "What's the matter with you!" he panted. "Can't you read? You can't park along here, and you're in the truck lane. Get going before the heavy work traffic piles up."

Greg explained the situation and pointed to the woman who was on the other side of the bridge rail.

Without a word the man ran back to his truck. In a few minutes he returned. He reached over the railing and helped Dave hang on to the woman, who was now loudly praying.

"I called a friend," the man whispered. "He'll have the police here soon."

"Lady," Dave addressed the distressed woman, "the Lord doesn't want you this way. He gave you life to cherish. Maybe you have troubles, but He will help you right here on earth."

"No, no!" the woman screamed. "He doesn't listen. He doesn't hear. I have to see Him face-to-face!"

"He listens, He hears," Dave said soothingly as Greg looked at his young friend in admiration. "He listens, but we don't always understand His answers. He has a plan for you, and you must live according to it. Wait and see. Have hope. Things will be better soon."

"No, no!" the woman cried again but in a much quieter tone. "I have had so much trouble. How long does it take? I can't stand this."

Dave went on in a calming tone. "The Lord never gives us more than we can bear. Come on, we will all help you. Come on now—let us help you."

The woman gradually quit struggling, and the truck driver helped Dave ease her back over the railing. She collapsed at their feet. The police arrived and quickly put a blanket over the sobbing woman.

"Good work," one of the officers said to the truck driver.

"I didn't do anything," he answered. "It was this young man who talked her out of jumping."

Dave laughed shakily. "He just called for help and then came back to help me. I could never have held on to her alone—she was so wild. Will she be all right now?"

"I hope so," the officer replied, looking at the woman as she was carried to the patrol car. "We'll do all we can for her."

After he had written down their names, the officer left. The boys tried to thank the trucker, but he just gave them a smart salute, saying, "It's all in a day's work!" and drove away.

"I don't know how you did it," Greg marveled. "How did you ever know what to say? I was afraid to even touch her!"

"Same here," Dave admitted. "But the poor woman needed help and needed it right away. How did I know what to say? The Lord guided me, that's how. I just prayed that she would understand me. The Lord always helps—He's our hope."

"Say, there must be more to this religious stuff than I thought," Greg admitted. "You know, I never did go to church much. Maybe you'll let me go with you sometime?"

"Be my guest!" Dave smiled. "And let's make that 'sometime' this week, huh?"

"Sure thing. Now we'd better get down to the motor vehicles office before they close."

"Not me!" Dave held out his shaking hands. "I

couldn't steer a kiddie car around the block right now."

Greg started for home. "Just call me when you're ready to go," he said. "You may drive my car anytime!"

16

Daddy

by Kitty Barron Thomas

C ome on, Mom," I pleaded. "I really don't have to go to school today. I would learn just as much by going to SeaWorld. Missing one day of school wouldn't be so bad!"

"No, Kitty. We'll only be going to show my friend Carol around. We won't stay long. We'll all go for the day when your father gets home. Now, find your sister, and both of you hurry to school before you're late." Mom was firm.

"Peggy, c'mon," I yelled glumly, "let's go!"

I was a sixth grader in the local church school. My family had lived in this southern California community a long time—nearly six months! That may not seem long to you, but for my family it was. You see, my father was an evangelist, and he held meetings in different cities across the country. Every six weeks or so, my mother, my sister, and I moved with him in our trailer house to a new place to start a new series of meetings.

In many ways it was exciting to be the daughter of an evangelist. Everywhere I went people treated me as if I were someone special. "You must be Elder Barron's daughter," someone would say. "You look just like him!"

I was so proud of him. He spent a lot of time away from us, but when he was home, we had fun. He took us places, such as Disneyland and SeaWorld—anywhere he thought we would enjoy ourselves. Sometimes after his long day of visiting with people and preaching at the meeting, I would rub his tired feet. He would sigh and tell me how wonderful it felt.

But today would change everything. Sitting in my desk that morning, I couldn't get my mind on schoolwork. I was supposed to be working on a geography report about Chile, but I kept thinking about SeaWorld. I was looking up some information about missionaries in Chile when my mother's friend Carol knocked on the classroom door.

Oh, great! I thought. *They've changed their minds and I get to go to SeaWorld after all.*

Carol talked quietly to my teacher for a minute, then called for me to come with her.

I was excited, but waited until we got outside before I asked. "Do I get to go to SeaWorld?"

She didn't answer.

"What's going on?" I searched her face carefully.

"Where do we go to get Peggy?" she asked in a quiet voice.

"Over there," I pointed.

When she didn't say another word, I began to worry. All the way home I watched cars racing by in every direction, just like always. Everything seemed the same, yet something was wrong. The closer we got to home, the more worried I became.

Peggy and I stepped into the house. Something was wrong. Very wrong. People were everywhere, and they were all crying. I started crying, too, though I didn't know why.

A woman put her arms around me and cried, "He was such a good daddy."

Then I knew. My father was not coming home. Ever.

I sat there in a daze while someone explained what had happened. Daddy loved flying. He had been a small airplane pilot for several years and had just recently purchased a new plane. He had taken some friends for a ride, and somehow something had gone wrong and the plane had crashed.

Now he was gone. I didn't have a father anymore. All around me sympathetic people were staring at me. But I wanted to be alone. I was too confused to handle it. I wanted them all to go away! Just when I thought I was going to explode, my friend Tammy came in and asked if I wanted to go for a walk.

We walked down the road by the dairy like we'd done many times before. We talked about school, our friends. Everyday things. We even joked and laughed. I began to relax a little, but it made me feel guilty.

"This isn't right," I told Tammy. "I shouldn't be

laughing. My father just died!"

"Your father wouldn't want you to be sad," Tammy disagreed. "He'd want you to keep on being happy."

When I got home, a crowd was still there and I didn't want to stay. "Mom, I want to go to my voice lesson," I told her as I hugged her. She looked so sad that I hugged her again.

"Are you sure you feel up to it?" she asked.

"Oh, yes, I'm fine. I'll feel better away from all these people."

"OK, dear. Handle it the best way you can." She smiled her understanding.

My lessons were with two other girls. We sang trios together. They were very surprised to see me. "Are you sure you want to practice?" they asked.

"I'm fine," I said. And I was. For a few minutes.

We sang several songs, and then the teacher picked out one I'd heard my father sing many times. As the teacher started to play, I could see my father singing, and then it all hit me. I would never hear him sing that song again. I would never hear him sing any song again. I felt a big lump swelling in my throat.

When it came time for me to sing, I couldn't. The tears I'd held back all day rolled down my face. The teacher took one look, handed me some tissues, and said it was OK for me to leave.

Once outside I let it all out. After crying for a while, I was able to do some serious thinking. What was life going to be like without Daddy? Why did God let him die? I needed him!

I had been walking, crying, and thinking for a long time when I realized I was home, and everyone was gone except my family. It was very quiet as I got ready for bed. Just a few hours ago my biggest problem had been not getting to go to SeaWorld. But now everything was so different.

Mother came in to kiss me good night. We cried together for a minute, and then I asked her, "What will I do without a father?"

She hugged me close and said, "You still have a Father. Your Father in heaven is still with you. He knows what has happened. He loves you very much. You'll have to learn to depend more on His love and protection."

Losing my father was a very bad experience. My life was never the same again. Many times I missed having him there as I got older and ran into problems. But I remembered what Mother told me and spent more time talking to my heavenly Father. I learned to trust Him with the problems I couldn't handle. Thanks to Him and the love of my mother, I made it.

I'll never forget my father, and someday in heaven we'll spend special time together again. I'm so glad I have that hope.

Mother was right. Losing Daddy wasn't what God wanted for my life, but He helped me through it and through the years since then. But through losing my father I learned something you should know too. Your Father in heaven will always love you. He will never leave you.

17

Mailed to Freedom

by William Cleveland

W ell, Henry, art thou ready?" The gray-bearded man spoke in a hushed voice.

"Yes sir, I think so." Henry sprang lightly into a wooden freight box that was only two feet eight inches wide, two feet deep, and three feet long.

He arranged himself and his legs in the small pile of straw placed in the bottom of the box to cushion him. At five feet ten inches and more than two hundred pounds, Henry had very little space for movement. "Lucky I'm not any taller," he laughed nervously.

Henry Brown, a young black man in his early thirties, was a slave. He worked on a plantation just west of Richmond, Virginia. He had decided to escape to freedom, to ride the Underground Railroad to the North—all the way to Canada, if necessary.

It was almost 1850, and before the decade ended, seventy-five thousand slaves would slip up North to freedom. They would be guided, sheltered, fed, and hidden by whites, most of whose names they would never know and whom they likely would never see again.

Most of those Underground Railroaders were church people. "God frowns when a man is held in bondage," they said. And they believed that whatever the risk, as Christians they must help these people escape.

And risk there certainly was! As more and more slaves escaped, the way became more and more dangerous.

Then one day Henry got a perfectly outrageous idea. "Put me in a large freight box and send me up to Philadelphia on the train. They never check shipments too carefully, you know." He chuckled. "You can just mail me north."

Now as little spikes of light slipped through cracks in the wall of the dusty livery stable, the men hurried about their final preparations. Outside, a sleepy-eyed man leaned back in a cane chair. Though you'd never have guessed it, he was the lookout. All his senses were tensed; he was ready to birdcall at the first sign of trouble.

A Quaker gentleman named Edward peered into the box. "Nay, nay, Henry, no good. Thou must stretch this way. Here, brace thy legs against yon wall. I tell thee, when this box is moved about, thou must hold absolutely still. It plainly says on the box that thou art 'dry goods,' and dry goods is not alive and doth not squirm about, mark ye."

Henry nodded grimly and shifted his position as he had been instructed.

"Now," the Quaker continued, "here be biscuits and a bladder of water. And here be a small hatchet to chop out with if anything goeth amiss. Likely this may take days; I know not exactly how many. But long as thou art moving now and then, things are still well."

Then the lid was fitted in place and nailed tightly shut. Poor Henry! It was nearly pitch-black in there. A few cracks and holes along the bottom let in air, but not much light. He grew more afraid. *Think about freedom*, he told himself. *Pray!*

Horses and wagon were led up to the sagging doors of the stable, and Henry's box along with two others just like it were loaded. All three boxes were well marked with "This side up with care" and "To Mr. William Still, Philadelphia."

Edward spoke again. "Men, we must keep watch, so wander over and pass time at the station. Oh, do not all go together! Dost thou wish to make every man in Richmond suspicious? Now remember, thou dost not know me and I know thee not—Robert! Wipe that smirk off thy face; this is no lark. There is danger here—for all of us."

It *was* dangerous. Slaveholders, angry over the rising number of escapes, had demanded new laws from Congress, and they'd gotten them. Anyone, white or black, caught helping a slave escape anywhere in the United States would be arrested on the spot. A heavy fine would have to be paid, and perhaps some time spent in jail. Some Underground Railroaders were even murdered in the night by shadowy night riders.

Young Robert turned the team and wagon toward the train station, humming nonchalantly as though he hadn't a care in the world. But his insides were quivery with fear.

"Hi, Mr. Adamson," he called out to the stationmaster. "Got three boxes of farm things to send to this here William Still in Philadelphia. Here's his address."

The stationmaster squinted at the paper. "Want 'em insured?"

"No, sir, no insurance."

"All right, set 'em over there. Joe!" Mr. Adamson yelled over his shoulder. "Give a hand over here."

Once the boxes were unloaded, Robert rode slowly back to the livery stable, glad his part was over. He saw two of his friends leaning against the station wall, watching out of the corners of their eyes. The most critical moment had arrived. If the boxes could be stamped and loaded onto the train without anyone finding out, it just might work.

With a grunt the stationmaster's men lifted Henry's box and carried it to the freight car. Henry went rigid. Not even daring to breathe, he braced himself and hunkered down in the blackness. They dropped the box on the freight car floor—upside down.

I'm going to be one big bruise if they don't learn to set this box down instead of dropping it, Henry thought.

But Henry was on the train! He heard the whistle

and felt the train lurch forward, picking up speed as it headed north. During the trip, which lasted twenty-seven hours, Henry's box was transported by wagon, railroad, steamboat, wagon again, railroad, ferry, railroad, and finally delivery wagon.

Despite the instructions on the box of "This side up with care," several times carriers placed the box upside-down, forcing Henry to ride that way for hours. He remained still and avoided detection.

He later wrote that his uncertain method of travel was worth the risk: "If you have never been deprived of your liberty, as I was, you cannot realize the power of that hope of freedom, which was to me indeed, an anchor to the soul both sure and steadfast."

William Still, who later would write *The Underground Railroad*, a book about the daring escapes of those days, paced the station platform in Philadelphia with his two friends. Concern showed in his eyebrows. For several days he'd been waiting for a special shipment from Richmond. Then he saw the boxes.

"Bring them around the side, if you please," Still asked the helpers. "My wagon is waiting there."

A half hour later he and his friends, safely hidden in an old toolshed, set to work with their crowbars. They opened the first box—machinery. Quickly they set to work on the second, and when they lifted the lid, out popped Henry, a huge grin covering his face. The first thing he did was recite a psalm from the Bible!

They hurried him off to a good meal, a hot tub, and a soft bed before sending him on to his new home.

Thanks to the help they were given, slaves were able to escape in many unusual ways. But perhaps none was quite as unusual as Henry's. He not only got his freedom that long-ago day; he got himself a lifelong nickname—Henry "Box" Brown, the man who was mailed to freedom.

18

Dr. Chin Is In

by Melanie Scherencel Hess

I couldn't put my finger on exactly when it happened. It was sort of like the gunk that builds up in your drainpipe. The sink begins to empty more and more slowly, until one day a tiny glob of tooth-paste finally stops up the whole works. Except that no amount of Mighty Mac Gunk Remover was going to get rid of the angry feelings that had built up between my dad and me.

I'd heard horror stories of unreasonable parents before. But now, misery of miseries, I actually owned one! I didn't know that my dad had an automated panic button until I became a teenager and it took effect. Just about the time the average kid hopes their father will become "Mr. Inconspicuous," my dad became "Mr. Attentive."

Well, not "Mr. Attentive," exactly. More like "Mr. Involved-in-Every-Aspect-of-Your-Life-So-You-Don't-

End-Up-in-Prison." I was mortified big-time. Every time I heard my name being called, it usually meant hearing one more chapter from that "Lessons Handed Down" manual they pass out to parents in the delivery room when you're born.

Take my sock drawer, for example. It was the perfect place to initiate a lecture.

"What a mess!" my dad would exclaim. "Some of these aren't even folded with their mates!"

"Come on, Dad," I'd moan. "If you don't like the way I fold my socks, can't you just stop looking in my sock drawer?"

"I was putting away your laundry. I didn't have a choice."

Aha! The age-old "just doing laundry" scam. I was convinced that he actually had a surveillance camera planted in my sock drawer so that he could immediately detect if any of my socks were carelessly mixed in with my underwear.

Those discussions would eventually cover everything from friends to clothes, until we'd finally deadlock. They always left me feeling as if somebody had shoved a chunk of lead into my chest.

Why couldn't things be like they used to be? Why did we have to fight all the time? Pretty soon we mostly ignored each other, and that was harder than the fighting.

Then one day Dad said we needed to talk. The air was thick with tension.

Here it comes, I thought. *I'll bet the United Nations*

never expected World War III to be initiated in our living room.

I expected him to drop a verbal bomb, like "You're grounded" or "Go clean your sock drawer," but he didn't.

"I'm going to see a Christian counselor," my dad said. "Do you want to come?"

It took a few moments, but finally I said, "OK."

When we got to Dr. Chin's office, I sat in the waiting room while my dad went in. Then it was my turn. Dr. Chin had a gentle face. He motioned for me to sit down. "Why are you here?" he asked kindly.

I fidgeted nervously. "I think it's my dad's way of telling me he thinks I'm a psychopath," I blurted. "Next stop, the mental ward."

Dr. Chin laughed. "You're not a psychopath . . . I don't think," he teased. "It's very normal for families to have bumpy places in their relationships. When you're having trouble handling it, it's a good idea to talk with someone like me who can see things from a neutral standpoint."

"Are you going to tell my dad what I say?"

"Not if you don't want me to," Dr. Chin reassured me.

I relaxed a little and slowly began telling Dr. Chin how I felt. He mostly nodded and took notes on his computer, asking me questions now and then.

"If both you and your dad want to fix this relationship, then God can help. After all, He created the whole idea of families in the first place."

"You mean there's hope for us?" I asked.

Dr. Chin smiled and answered my question with another one. "Do you love your dad?"

"Yeah," I answered.

"Have you told him that lately?" Dr. Chin asked.

"No, I guess I haven't much felt like it."

"That might be a good place to start." Dr. Chin leaned back in his chair. "Your dad has always taken care of you. Maybe he feels a little left out now that you're gaining independence. He'll deal with it eventually."

Wow! I thought. *Maybe there is a ray of hope for us. After all, this guy seems to know what he's talking about.*

"I suspect," Dr. Chin was continuing, "it might help if you gave your dad some reassurance that he's still loved."

"I'll try," I smiled.

The ride home was quiet, and I thought about what Dr. Chin had said. I'd been so caught up in my own independence thing, I'd all but forgotten that Dad had feelings too.

"Did you like Dr. Chin?" my dad asked.

"Yeah," I said. "I wouldn't mind talking to him again."

"Me either." Dad smiled.

"You know"—I chose my words carefully—"I think if you gave me a little more space and trust—"

"Yes? Go on," said Dad, obviously interested.

"I'd feel like being more open with you about what's going on in my life." The glimmer of hope was growing brighter.

"I could work with you on that," Dad agreed.

Wow! Big glimmers of hope for us!

"Uh, Dad? Does that mean you're going to take your surveillance camera out of my sock drawer?" I teased.

His eyes widened. "How did you know?"

We both laughed.

Dad let out a deep sigh of relief. "This is starting to feel a whole lot better, kiddo. Is there anything else you have on your mind?"

"Yep," I nodded.

"Let's have it—I'm man enough to take it."

"Dad . . . I love you."

"I love you too," my dad repeated.

When we stopped at Taco Delite for a quick supper, we gave each other a big hug before going in. Yep, there sure *was* hope for us!

No, it still isn't happily ever after all the time. But between Dad, me, and God—with a little more help from Dr. Chin (I call him God's Awesome Gunk Remover)—things are getting a whole lot better.

19

Cindy's Night of Fright

by Judy L. Shull

Enough horsing around, boys," Mrs. Shull said as she took her turn in front of the bathroom mirror.

Eric and Adam wandered out to the kitchen to find their school shoes.

A few minutes later Mrs. Shull heard a scuffle in the hallway. Looking out the bathroom door, she said suddenly, "Eric! Adam! That is enough!"

"What?" the boys said in unison, causing a wave of giggles to overtake them.

"Boys, you have mud on your shoes, and now it's all over the carpet! Why do you think we had you leave your shoes in the kitchen?"

"Oh, sorry," Eric said. Adam just looked down at his feet.

"Take your shoes out to the deck and try to stomp the dirt off," their mother instructed.

The boys noisily lumbered out the back door and onto the deck. Suddenly Adam yelled, "Mom! *Mom!*"

Now what? their mother thought, imagining that she would never be able to get ready for work.

"Mom! Cindy's in the pool!" Adam cried, racing back into the house.

Quickly Mrs. Shull ran out to the deck. The family's golden retriever, Cindy, was paddling around in the pool!

Mrs. Shull ran to the edge of the pool. "Poor Cindy!" she said as the dog tried to stay afloat in the above-ground pool.

Cindy began paddling toward the sound of Mrs. Shull's voice. Mrs. Shull leaned over and, with her best lifesaving lift, pulled the wet, heavy dog from the pool.

"Oh, Cindy," she said, "are you OK?"

Cindy's eyes had a glazed look. Ever so slowly the dog walked down the steps of the deck and out into the yard.

Eric appeared around the side of the house. "I was going to get the pool ladder," he informed his mom.

"Thanks, Eric, but she's already out. Please go and check her food bowl."

Eric strolled over to the dish and then announced, "It's full."

"Boys, that means Cindy's been in the pool all night! Otherwise she would have eaten her dinner for sure. Adam, get the rugs out of the bathroom. We're going to need to get Cindy in the tub and warm her up."

Cindy followed the family into the house. She even

did what she was told! Normally, once plopped in the bathtub, Cindy would jump back out. This time she sat down.

Turning on the shower faucets, Mrs. Shull let the warm water flow over Cindy's cold body.

A few minutes later Mrs. Shull turned off the water. "I think she's as warm as we're going to get her for now. Let's dry her off."

With a great deal of effort they got the wet dog up on her feet and began drying Cindy off. When the dog was toweled off, Mrs. Shull lifted her onto the towel-covered sleeping mat that Eric had brought into the bathroom. Cindy stood on the mat, then stretched out and lay down on it.

"We'll call the vet when his office opens. But for now we'll let Cindy get some sleep. I don't know how she managed to survive dog-paddling in the pool all night."

Later that morning, after talking to the vet, they learned they had done the right thing for their dog. Now the family needed to watch Cindy and make sure she was getting enough to eat and drink, along with plenty of rest.

That evening Eric asked his dad, "Do you have any idea how Cindy was able to survive all night trying to stay afloat in that cold pool?"

"Well," Mr. Shull said, "I think it might have to do with hope."

Eric and Adam thought a moment. Then Adam said, "You mean Cindy lived all night swimming in the pool because she thought we might save her?"

"I think so," Mr. Shull replied. "I think she had hope of being rescued, so she didn't give up."

"Cool," Eric said.

"We need hope, too, boys," Mr. Shull said, reaching for his Bible. "Listen to what Jeremiah 17:7 has to say: 'Blessed is the man who trusts in the LORD, and whose hope is the LORD.' It's because we have the hope God gives us through Jesus that we're able to keep going."

Dad hugged each of the boys. "Cindy—and the Bible—have sure taught us some amazing things, haven't they?"

Both boys nodded their heads, and Cindy seemed to wag her tail in agreement.

20

In Love With a Birdbrain

by Heather Grovet

The sound came from a grimy heap in the corner of the shop. I bent over, trying to see what had made the noise.

There it was—a young sparrow, not old enough to fly, covered with dust. It cowered in the corner, only its chest moving as it panted nervously.

"Silly thing," I muttered, wondering what to do with it. Overhead, the rafters echoed with loud chirps from older and wiser sparrows. Its mother was probably up there watching us. Surely she'd take care of it, even if the little bird had been dumb enough to fall out of the nest.

Then something rubbed against my leg. I looked down and saw our striped tomcat, Sparkle. He purred cheerfully, but I wasn't happy to see him. I was sure a helpless baby bird would make a perfect cat snack.

Pushing Sparkle aside, I reached under the pile of

boxes. The small creature didn't move, even when my hands came around it.

Now what? I knew what my dad would say when I turned up with the bird. My dad hates sparrows. He had built this new shop planning to store his vehicles and equipment inside. But sparrows decided it was the perfect birdhouse. Hundreds of them lived in the rafters and messed all over the equipment. My dad threatened their lives each day.

"Just wait until I get that overhead door in place," he'd warn the birds. "Then you're in trouble."

He wasn't going to be the least bit happy about one of the enemies moving into our house.

Once inside, I had a better look at the sparrow. It was frightened and hunched down in my hand as though it thought it could make itself small enough to disappear. The creature was a mishmash of dirty tones: dark-brown feathers with creamy-brown lines. As I watched, its yellowish beak opened, and out came an amazingly shrill "Peep!" It sat quietly for a moment, then began to screech. "Peep! Peep! Peep!"

How could a bird only a few inches tall make such a loud noise? Obviously I wouldn't be able to hide it from my parents!

Luckily my mom is a real animal lover. After I told her the story, she phoned around, trying to get some ideas of what to feed a baby sparrow. When she got off the phone, she shook her head.

"Looks as though no one else knows either," Mom said with a frown. "I guess we'll just have to use some common sense." Mom told me that sparrows eat seeds, grains, and little bugs. "We'll try to feed it those kinds of things."

"Mom! You want me to catch bugs?" I asked.

"You've got it," she answered with a faint smile. "If you're going to be this little birdbrain's mother, you'll have to find it something to eat."

The name "Birdbrain" stuck. And suddenly I became a mother bird. We fed Birdbrain all sorts of things, such as oatmeal porridge with dead flies mixed in, dog food, and hard-boiled eggs.

At first Birdbrain was difficult to feed. The creature cowered down low whenever I came near. I had to pry its beak open and stuff a few crumbs into it. But within a few hours a little light seemed to come on inside its birdy head. Birdbrain took a good look at me and decided I was Mama.

By evening all I had to do was walk by its cage, and Birdbrain's head would pop up and its bright-yellow beak would open. I used a plastic spoon to scoop in a few bites of some sort of mush. Birdbrain loved it. Before long, whenever the plastic spoon appeared, Birdbrain would dance around in circles, head outstretched and beak flapping. More than once the bird fell right off my knee.

Within a few days the little creature began fluttering around. Birdbrain could fly a few inches from the perch to my knee. It liked to be close to me.

One afternoon Dad sat with his fingers in his ears, watching me feed Birdbrain. When I was finished,

Dad smiled. "You know," he said, "I don't think this bird fell from a nest. I think its mother pushed it out!"

I had to smile too. If I were a mother sparrow and had a half dozen noisy babies to feed, I'd probably be tempted to push a few out of the nest myself! But even though Birdbrain was noisy, a lot of work, and not even that nice-looking with its porridge-encrusted chest and neck, I still loved my feathery "baby."

Finally the day came for Birdbrain to return to the wild. I carried it to the shop and set my winged friend on a ledge. "I'll be back later," I said.

I was hoping that Birdbrain would eventually decide to be a bird and follow the other birds in their hunt for food. But until then, I planned to come down to the shop every few hours and offer Birdbrain something to eat.

At first things happened the way I planned. Birdbrain rushed over to me whenever I came to visit. The food I brought was eagerly devoured. But Birdbrain also seemed happy to hang out with the other birds. Maybe things were working out after all.

But then one morning no Birdbrain appeared. And when I went out at dinner my beloved bird wasn't there either. By evening I was worried. Was Birdbrain dead, or alive somewhere living a normal bird life?

I never learned what happened to Birdbrain. A few weeks later I found a dead sparrow in our yard. I looked at it carefully, but I couldn't tell if it was Birdbrain. The multicolored brown tones and the yellow beak were the same on millions of other sparrows.

I missed my little Birdbrain. I know it was just a sparrow, but it was my sparrow. I think Birdbrain loved me, and I loved Birdbrain, noise and mess and all.

After my weeks with Birdbrain, I could better understand what Jesus said in Luke 12:6: "Are not five sparrows sold for two pennies? Yet not one of them is forgotten by God" (NIV).

Sparrows are everywhere. They're noisy and a bother, and they're worth nothing in the eyes of humans. But God made them, and He loves them, and He remembers each one of them.

If God loves sparrows, think how much He loves us. Even when I'm like Birdbrain, noisy and dirty and pesky, I'm still loved by God. And I know He loves you too.

The Silent Culprit

by Sari Fordham

"Who broke the eyedropper?" Mr. Gillham asked. He held the incriminating evidence in front of our sixth-grade class. His voice was serious, his eyebrows raised inquiringly.

Nobody answered. The silence was so powerful that it almost became a noise. Todd and Jason, the two class clowns, shifted uncomfortably in their seats. It seemed as if everyone was waiting for one of them to confess.

Everyone except me. I sat in the back row next to Todd. I was the quiet girl. The A student. The one teachers loved to place next to troublemakers. In short, I was the least likely suspect. Nobody even noticed as I nibbled uncomfortably on my bottom lip.

I had broken the eyedropper during science class. We were working on an experiment involving acids and bases. My group had sent me to get the equipment.

I had grabbed the ill-fated instrument and accidentally dropped it. No one seemed to have noticed. Without a second thought, I had put it back in the box and grabbed another. I didn't even consider telling Mr. Gillham. After all, it was just an eyedropper.

Now I tapped my feet on the gray tile floor and wondered what to do. *Never in a million years will someone think it's you,* a voice seemed to whisper in my ear. *And it's not as though you did it on purpose.* I gazed at my folded hands and said nothing.

"It's not just an eyedropper," Mr. Gillham said, looking slowly around the room. "This is a matter of honesty."

Oh no, I thought. *I certainly can't confess now. Everyone will think I'm a liar. Oh, I hope no one finds out I did it!*

"I'm sorry to say this," Mr. Gillham continued, "but we will stop working on the science experiment until someone confesses." He put down the eyedropper and picked up our English textbook. The class moaned.

At recess my friends huddled in a group. "Those boys are such jerks," Joanna said. "They should just confess. We all know who did it." She cast a dark eye at Jason and Todd as they stood on the baseball field playing catch.

Without answering, I bent down and hastily retied my shoelaces.

The question of what to do loomed over me like one of those cartoon thunderstorms. I struggled throughout the rest of the day. I did poorly on a social studies quiz. I couldn't concentrate in math.

By now I desperately wanted to say something. I had given a hundred imaginary confessions in my head. But each time I decided to approach Mr. Gillham, I was filled with doubt. What would he think of me? What would the class think? As long as I kept quiet, everyone would continue believing that I was a good person.

When I got home that afternoon, my older sister Sonja took one look at me and asked, "What's the matter? Something happen at school today?"

"It's nothing," I replied, flopping down on the couch.

"Try me," Sonja said.

I took a deep breath and told her the whole story. "So anyway," I finished with a melodramatic sigh, "I just don't know what to do."

"Come on," Sonja said. At fifteen, she liked being the expert. "You totally know what to do. The question is—how long are you going to torture yourself?"

I stared down at my chewed fingernails and said nothing.

"How about this?" Sonja said. "I'll find Mr. Gillham's phone number, and you can call him now."

"Call his house?" my voice squeaked. My eyebrows shot up in alarm. But Sonja didn't seem to notice. She was too busy flipping through the phone book.

"Here it is," she said triumphantly. She circled his number and handed me the book. When she finally noticed my look of panic, her face melted. "OK, let's practice. Pretend I'm Mr. Gillham."

We rehearsed several times. Then, with a shaking hand, I dialed the number. *Oh, I hope Mr. Gillham will forgive me!* I thought. He answered the phone with a cheery hello.

"Hi, Mr. Gillham," I said. "This is, um, this is Sari."

"Hi, Sari." His voice was pleasant. "What can I do for you?"

"Well," I stammered. Now that the moment of truth had arrived, it was worse than I had imagined. My palms were sweaty. My voice trembled. My heart felt as if it were going to leap out of my body. I began to realize what a big deal an eyedropper could be.

"I just called to tell you that I broke the eyedropper." Now that I had begun, the words tumbled faster and faster. "I'm really sorry. I didn't mean to. It was an accident. I should have told you, but I didn't think it mattered, and then I was too embarrassed. I'm so sorry. I'll pay for it. I'm sorry. I hope you can forgive me." I forced myself to stop talking.

"Thanks for telling me, Sari," Mr. Gillham said kindly. "I really appreciate it. I'm sure it was an accident. So let's not worry about this anymore."

When I got off the phone, I was grinning.

"See. I told you," Sonja said. This time I didn't even care if she was right.

Mr. Gillham could have told me that my silence was a lie. He could have told me that by not speaking out, I was giving other people a bad name. He could have reminded me that even small things are a big deal if we have to hide our actions. But I guess he knew he didn't have to. I had already learned the hard way.

22

Marooned
on Wreck Rock

by Ron Reese

O *oo-ooh, ooo-ooh,* howled the wind along the beach.

Twelve-year-old Tom Harvey listened as the waves crashed against the shore that bleak Sunday morning, July 13, 1828. Tom and his family lived on a tiny island off the coast of Newfoundland called Isle aux Morts, which means "Island of the Dead."

"Where are you going on a day like this?" he asked his sister Ann.

"I love to watch the waves crash up on the sand," replied his sister.

Tom watched as she walked away. Not long afterward she came running back down the beach.

"What's the hurry, Ann?" he asked.

"Where's Father?" she gasped.

"He's inside with Mother," Tom replied, wondering what was wrong with his sister. He didn't have long to wonder, because moments later Ann and their father burst through the doorway of their house.

"Come along, Tom!" called his father as they ran toward the beach. Tom followed, really curious now. He had never seen his fifty-six-year-old father run this fast.

Ssseeet, ssseeet! whistled his father. "Come, Hairyman! Come!" Hairyman was the family dog, a large, black Newfoundland.

"Rrrffff! Rrrffff!" barked their dog as he joined the three on their race toward the beach.

"Quick, children, into the boat!" directed Mr. Harvey.

Tom could control his curiosity no longer. "Father, where are we going? And why?" he puffed as he and his sister stepped off the wharf into the family's twelve-foot fishing boat, which was rising and falling with the ocean waves.

"We're on a rescue mission, Tom," shouted his father above the roar of the waves. "And we haven't a moment to lose."

His father stepped into the rear of the boat, and Hairyman jumped into the bow. After Tom and his sister untied the boat from the wharf, the boy and his father rowed the boat straight into the waves and out to sea.

Seeing her younger brother's questioning look, Ann filled Tom in on the details. "I had gone only a short way down the beach when I noticed a wooden barrel and a mattress floating toward shore."

Tom needed no more explanation. These items floating in the water could mean only one thing. Somewhere offshore a ship had sunk. And the four of them were now on a rescue mission in choppy water they wouldn't normally take their boat into.

"Let's row along the beach so we can see if any survivors made it ashore," Tom's father instructed.

Suddenly they spotted something on the sand. Drawing closer, they saw six men who had survived the wreck and made it to shore.

"Thank God you're all safe," said Mr. Harvey as they landed their punt. "How many were on board? Do you think there are other survivors?"

"Who can tell?" moaned one of the men. "We did notice a small island off to our right as we swam to shore. Perhaps others are there."

Tom's family knew the island well. Situated three miles from shore, it had been named Wreck Rock for obvious reasons.

As they set off for Wreck Rock, Tom could hear his father above the sound of the crashing waves: "God, if there are any more survivors, please help us find them."

Finally Tom could see the tiny island, no bigger than most houses. Straining his eyes, he saw that nearly two hundred people—men, women, and children—were stranded there. All were waving their hands wildly at the family in the tiny boat.

The closest the Harveys could get to the island was about one hundred feet because the wind and waves kept pushing them backward toward their home.

Finally his father called out, "Tom, hand me that chunk of wood in the back of the boat."

Tom wasn't sure what his father would need a chunk of wood for, but he handed it to him. As Tom and his sister kept trying to row the boat forward just to keep it from floating backward, their father heaved the small log toward the tiny isle.

The men on shore tied a piece of rope to the wood. A man then tried swimming toward the boat while holding on to the wood. Others behind him held on to the end of the rope.

Tom patted Hairyman, who was sitting by him in the boat. "Boy, you'd like to help, wouldn't you?"

Just then Mr. Harvey called, "Go fetch the stick, Hairyman! Go fetch the stick!"

Tom was amazed to see their dog plunge into the choppy water and dog-paddle toward the man holding the wood. Hairyman grabbed the wood while the man held on to the rope. The dog then swam back toward the bobbing boat, towing the man with him.

"Tom, keep rowing while Ann and I pull this man in," urged his father.

Tom strained at the oars to keep the craft steady while his father and his seventeen-year-old sister pulled the wet man into the boat.

"It worked!" The man sounded excited. Then he lay down exhausted.

Tom's father threw the log back toward the island. The men ashore pulled the log in for the next rescue effort. Hairyman kept watching the large chunk of wood.

"Go get it!" called Tom. "Go fetch the stick."

This time a woman picked up the two-foot log and made her way into the water. Right away Hairyman grabbed the log and towed her to the boat, while she held the rope.

Again and again this procedure was repeated for the rest of that day, the next day, and the day after that. During that time Tom, Ann, their father, and the dog were able to rescue 163 people. They turned out to be immigrants from Ireland who were moving to Canada.

But Tom and his family weren't finished helping the survivors yet.

Because there wasn't enough housing on Isle aux Morts, the Harveys helped some of the men build large lean-tos.

Food was another scarcity. Though there were eight children in Tom's family, his parents shared all they had with the Irish immigrants. Tom didn't know what they would do when the food ran out, but he knew enough to trust in God.

Fortunately the HMS *Tyne* arrived eight days later to transport the survivors onward to Halifax, Nova Scotia. Once Captain Grant of the rescue ship found out there were no provisions left on the island for the Harveys and the other inhabitants, he ordered that the people's bread and flour supplies be replenished from the provisions on board his ship. Tom could certainly see the Lord's leading there.

And sometime later Lloyd's of London gave the Harveys a check for one hundred pounds for their self-less heroism! They had depended on God and hoped He would provide for everyone—and He did.

23

Never Give Up

by Renee Coffee

Scientists put a group of rats into a water tank and watched to see how long they would swim. The rats paddled around for seventeen minutes before they gave up.

The tired rats were taken out and a new group put in the water. After a few minutes, the new group was taken out for a short time, and then returned to the water.

The second group of rats easily passed the seventeen-minute mark set by the first group. When the stopwatch reached seventeen hours, they were still paddling around. It took thirty-six hours of swimming to finally wear out the second group of rats.

Why did one group last only seventeen minutes, while the other group swam for thirty-six hours? What made the difference?

The second group had something the first group

didn't have. They had hope. Since they had been able to escape the water once, they believed in their tiny rat brains that it could happen again. So they kept swimming.

Hope is what made the difference. And hope is what makes the difference for all of us who are waiting for Jesus' second coming.

Ever since Jesus went back to heaven nearly two thousand years ago, Christians have been waiting for Him to return. But some lost hope and stopped believing when His return was delayed.

If we study the Bible and keep in contact with Jesus through prayer, we'll find the assurance we need to keep believing. Hope will get us through the discouraging times and help us continue our incredible journey until Jesus comes back and rescues us.

24

Last Memory

by Erin Beers

I breathed in the fresh salty air as my hand rested on the smooth white paddleboard. As I pushed down, trying to steady myself, the board started to tilt, just like before. I reached for the other side, hoping to gain some control of the board. It was too late, and the board flipped over—again. Tears threatened my eyes, but the soft ocean wind calmed me. Folding my arms across my chest, I didn't want to even try it again.

"One more time; you can do this," my brother, Christopher, encouraged, staring at me with confident eyes while handing me the paddleboard.

My head protested, but I found myself reaching for the board. My hands rested on the board, and this time two sturdy hands were at my waist. As Christopher supported me, I pushed myself out of the water. Soon both knees rested on the board. I was grateful for my brother's strong hands, which felt like a force field blocking out anything harmful. Then Christopher let go and . . . I was balancing!

"I knew you could—" But his words were quickly cut off as my tidal wave of failure smacked him in the face.

The horrible taste of saltwater entered my mouth. Now I was officially soaked and doubly discouraged. I brushed my tangled brown hair out of my face to glance at Christopher, expecting him to be just as furious with my fall as I was. But he wasn't; he just laughed it off. The look of worry that had been on my face left, and a warm smile replaced it.

"So close," Christopher encouraged. "Try it again. I bet you can stand up this time." His teeth sparkled and his arm flexed to push the paddleboard closer to me.

I gritted my teeth, trying to keep a smile on my face. I agreed to try it again. I closed my eyes, took in a deep breath, and told myself, *I can do this. I'm not going to fall. I'm going to show Christopher that I can learn to ride a paddleboard.*

I bravely moved my foot forward through the clear water. I reached out, my hands sliding down the board and stopping in the middle.

As I mounted the board, it tipped slightly from the weight of my body. I glanced at a school of fish as they darted away to avoid the commotion.

OK, now I just have to get up and balance myself, I reasoned. *But how?* I tried to remember what little bit I'd already learned. Still on my stomach, my lips pinched together, I was frustrated with myself for not being able to think of how to stand up!

"As soon as you're comfortable, try kneeling. Then when you think you're ready, just stand up," Christopher instructed.

"How?" I muttered. "I always fall!"

"Let me see the board." Christopher stepped closer to me and reached for the paddleboard.

I reluctantly slid off as Christopher mounted the board. He grabbed both sides and shot out of the water. After kneeling on the board, he was soon standing, making it look simple.

It's not fair! I complained inwardly. *I tried the same thing, but it didn't work for me!* I felt a tear stream down my cheek. My hand instinctively wiped it away before anyone could notice.

Christopher dismounted the board and said, "Don't beat yourself up. You'll just get more frustrated, and then you'll never learn." He jumped off the board, splashing me in the process.

I wiped my face and stepped forward. *This time for sure*, I told myself. I gently touched the board, then shot out of the water just like Christopher had shown me. This time I landed on my knees. I lifted up my foot, only to have the board shake. I quickly lifted my other foot, and suddenly . . . I was standing! I was actually standing on the paddleboard!

"I did it! I'm balancing!" I screeched excitedly.

"I knew you could do it," Christopher responded. "Now stay up while I get you the paddle."

Clouds drifted closer to the sun. I didn't pay much

attention to them, though, because I was focused on Christopher, who had gone to fetch the paddle that had drifted away a bit. He retrieved it, then handed it to me. Excited, I leaned over to grab it. The board wobbled, but Christopher grabbed the board and steadied it.

"Careful," he said, smiling. He handed me the paddle again, then let go of the board.

A smile spread across my face as I regained my balance. I dipped the paddle in the water on my right side and pushed it back. Then I repeated the action on my left side. Little ripples spread through that water behind me. I was moving. I was paddleboarding!

The clouds now completely covered the sun. *Boom!* I jumped, almost losing my balance. Thunder roared in the distance, and lightning soon danced across the sky. *This can't be happening!* I thought. *It's not even noon!*

"Erin, let's go," called Christopher.

I slowly turned to make my way toward shore. The sun still shone on the beach, but behind me a fierce storm brewed.

I knew my brother would need to head back to college in a little while. "No, I don't want you to leave!" I cried.

When we were ready to part ways, Christopher shuffled over to give me his precious goodbye hug.

"I wish you could stay a little longer," I told him. I looked at the ground, noticing his bare feet and the few grains of sand still stuck to them.

"Me too," he said, "but I can't." Once again his

sunburned arms opened wide, and he wrapped them around me. I buried my head in his gray T-shirt and swung my arms around him.

Too soon he pulled away from me. "Take care of Mom for your favorite brother, OK?" He raised his eyebrows slightly, and his blue eyes pleaded for my consent.

"I'll try," I promised.

With that, Christopher turned and headed for his car. Before he drove off he waved one last time.

"I love you," I whispered as his car shrunk from my view. I didn't bother to wipe away my tears as they poured down my cheeks.

I wish this story had a different ending, but that wasn't the last time I cried for Christopher. As it turned out, that day was the last time I saw him alive. My dear brother died on December 26, 2012, and I still miss him.

But the memory of his kindness lives on. And I'm confident that one day I'll see his dazzling smile and mischievous blue eyes in heaven. Now I just try to keep my balance in this sinful, dangerous world as I live in hope to see him again.

25

A Speck of Hope

by Diane Stark

Do you want to go for a walk?" Emma asked Mom one afternoon.

Mom frowned. "It looks like it's going to rain."

"I don't care. I need to talk about everything, and I don't want anyone to overhear what I'm saying."

Mom nodded, and minutes later they were on their way. Emma glanced up at the dark-gray sky. "Wow, you weren't kidding about the rain," she said. "It's all right, though. The day just matches my mood."

"I understand, honey," Mom said. "Our family has had a really rough few months."

For the next hour Mom and Emma talked through some of the troubles their family had been experiencing. Emma's grandpa had suffered another stroke, and this one had left him unable to walk and had caused him to have memory loss.

"He usually can't even remember my name, Mom,

and it really hurts my feelings," Emma said.

"I know this is hard. You and Grandpa have always been especially close, and watching him get sicker and sicker is really tough."

Emma wiped her eyes. "I'm worried about what is going to happen with Dad's job too."

When Emma's grandpa had gotten so sick, Emma's dad had taken time off from his job to help take care of Grandpa. Dad's boss had been understanding at first, but now he said that if Dad took any more days off, he'd have to step down from his management position, and that would mean a much smaller paycheck. Emma knew that her family couldn't afford that.

"I'm scared about that, too, honey," Mom admitted. "We depend on Dad's paycheck, but right now Grandma and Grandpa depend on us. It's such a difficult situation."

Emma swallowed hard so she wouldn't cry. "My grades aren't very good this year either," she said. "It's hard to concentrate with all of these other worries."

Mom put her arm around Emma's shoulder. "I know, honey. It'll be OK. All of it will be OK."

"I'm really struggling to believe that right now," Emma said as her tears finally fell. "I feel as if I'm losing hope."

Mom's eyebrows shot up. "You're losing hope? But you're an optimist. You've always been so cheerful, no matter what is going on."

Emma shrugged. "It's too much all at once. Grandpa being sick, Dad's job, me struggling in school. It's too much for me to handle."

"I know it's a lot, but God will help you with your problems if you ask Him."

"Can we pray?"

"Now?"

"Yes, now."

So right there on the side of the road Mom and Emma stopped and joined hands.

"Lord, we don't have a plan here," Mom prayed. "We don't know what's going to happen with any of these situations. It's scary, but we trust Your plan. We know that You love us and that You want the best for us."

"Help me, Lord," Emma said through her tears. "Help me to trust You and to remember that You are in control. And that alone should give me hope."

They prayed for Grandpa, Dad's job, and Emma's grades, and then they said "Amen."

Emma raised her head and looked up at the sky. The dark clouds covered the entire sky, and she knew they'd be lucky to make it home before the downpour started. But then something caught her eye. A small hole in the clouds with the prettiest blue peeking through.

"Do you see that?" Mom asked.

Emma nodded. "It wasn't there before we prayed."

As Emma stared at the speck of blue in that sky of gray, she felt a peace come over her. "Everything is going to be all right," she said. "I trust God and His plan for us."

Emma pulled out her cell phone and snapped a picture of the sky. She knew that the days ahead might be hard, and she wanted a reminder that when we have God, we always have hope.

GUIDE'S GREATEST . . .

Made any good discoveries lately?

Guide's Greatest Discovery Stories
Lori Peckham, editor

Discoveries can be big or small—but they're always exciting!

In *Guide's Greatest Discovery Stories* you'll find out what happens when Mother opens the front door to discover a rattlesnake on her doorstep; and what do the three rough-looking strangers really want on board the missionary boat? Joseph doesn't believe the rumors of a haunted house, but what are those noises in the night, and who is climbing the stairs toward him?

Yes, discoveries may be big or small, but sometimes they can lead to making important decisions between right and wrong. Paperback, 160 Pages • 978-0-8163-6260-8

Collect them all!

Pacific Press®
Publishing Association

"Where the Word is life"

Three ways to order:
1 Local	Adventist Book Center®
2 Call	1-800-765-6955
3 Shop	AdventistBookCenter.com

 AdventistBookCenter.com   AdventistBookCenter    @AdventistBooks   AdventistBooks